ESSENTIAL
GNOSTIC
SCRIPTURES

ESSENTIAL GNOSTIC SCRIPTURES

Willis Barnstone
and Marvin Meyer

SHAMBHALA
Boston & London
2010

Shambhala Publications, Inc.
Horticultural Hall
300 Massachusetts Avenue
Boston, Massachusetts 02115
www.shambhala.com

9 8 7 6 5 4 3 2 1

First edition
Printed in the United States of America

∞This edition is printed on acid-free paper that meets the
American National Standards Institute z39.48 Standard.
♻This book was printed on 30% postconsumer recycled paper.
For more information please visit www.shambhala.com.

Distributed in the United States by Random House, Inc.,
and in Canada by Random House of Canada Ltd

Library of Congress Cataloging-in-Publication Data
Essential gnostic scriptures/[compiled by] Willis Barnstone and
Marvin Meyer.—1st ed.
p. cm.
Includes bibliographical references.
ISBN 978-1-59030-549-2 (hardcover: alk. paper)   1.Gnosticism.
I. Barnstone, Willis, 1927– II. Meyer, Marvin.
BT1390.E86 2010
299'.932—dc22
2010023009

CONTENTS

ESSENTIAL
GNOSTIC
SCRIPTURES

INTRODUCTION

MARVIN MEYER

Gnosis and Gnostics

The religious mystics designated as gnostics were spiritual people who announced a way of salvation through gnosis, or knowledge. They proclaimed that a person should know oneself, should know the inner person, and thereby gnostic men and women may come to a direct knowledge of god.[1] With such gnosis, people could experience freedom and independence from the mediation of rabbis, priests, bishops, imams, or other authorities. Religious authorities were not pleased, and they condemned the gnostics as heretics, threats to the well-being of organized religion. In particular, heresiologists—heresy hunters who attempted to expose people considered dangerous to the Christian masses—fulminated against what they maintained was the falsehood of the gnostics. Still, from the challenge of this perceived threat came a great deal of the theological reflection that has characterized the intellectual history of the Christian church.

The historical roots of the gnostics reach back into the time of the Greeks, Romans, and Second Temple Jews. Some gnostics were Jewish, others Greco-Roman, and many were Christian. There were Mandaean gnostics from Iraq and Iran; Manichaeans from Europe, the Middle East, North Africa, and all the way to China; Islamic gnostics in the Muslim world; and Cathars in western Europe. The heyday of their influence extends from the second century c.e. through the next several centuries. Their influence and their presence, some say, continue to the present day.

Gnostics sought knowledge and wisdom from many different sources, and they accepted insight wherever it could be found. Like those who came before them, they embraced wisdom, Sophia, understood variously and often taken as the personified manifestation of divine insight. To gain knowledge of the deep things of god, gnostics read and studied diverse religious and philosophical texts. In addition to Jewish sacred literature, Christian documents, and Greco-Roman religious and philosophical texts, gnostics studied religious works from the Egyptians, Mesopotamians, Zoroastrians, Muslims, and Buddhists. All such sacred texts disclosed truths, and all were to be celebrated for their wisdom.

Gnostics loved to explore who they were and where they had come from, and hence they read creation stories such as the opening chapters of Genesis with vigor and enthusiasm. Like other interpreters, they recognized that creation stories not only claim to describe what *was* once upon a time, but also suggest what *is* now, in our own world. The gnostics carried to their reading a conviction that the story of creation was not a happy one. There is, they reasoned, something fundamentally wrong with the world, there is too much evil and pain and death in the world, and so there must have been something wrong with creation.

Consequently, gnostics provided innovative and oftentimes disturbing interpretations of the creation stories they read. They concluded that a distinction, often a dualistic distinction, must be made between the transcendent, spiritual deity, who is surrounded by heavenly entities known as aeons and who is all wisdom and light, and the creator of the world, who is at best incompetent and at worst malevolent. Yet through everything, they maintained, a spark of transcendent knowledge, wisdom, and light persists within people who are in the know. The transcendent deity is the source of that enlightened life and light. The meaning of the creation drama, when properly understood, is that human beings—gnostics in particular—derive their knowledge and light from the transcendent god, but through the mean-spirited actions of the demiurge, the creator of the world, they have been confined within this world. (The Platonic aspects of this imagery are apparent.) Humans in this world are imprisoned, asleep, drunken, fallen, ignorant. They need to find themselves—to be freed, awakened, made sober, raised, and enlightened. In other words, they need to return to gnosis.

This distinction between a transcendent god and the creator of the world is all the more remarkable when it is recalled that many of the earliest gnostic thinkers who made such a distinction seem to have been Jews. What might have led them to such a conclusion that seems to fly in the face of Jewish monotheistic affirmations? Could it have been the experience of the political and social trauma of the time, culminating in the destruction of the Second Temple in 70 C.E., that prompted serious reflection upon the problem of evil and stimulated the production of Jewish apocalyptic compositions? Could it have been the reflection of Hellenistic Jewish thinkers who were schooled in Judaica and Greek philosophy and recognized the deep philosophical and theological issues surrounding the transcendence of the high god and the need for cosmic intermediaries to be involved with this world? Could it have been that among the creative Jewish minds, representative of the rich diversity of Judaism during the first centuries before and of the Common Era, who boldly addressed the real challenges of Jewish mysticism before Kabbalah, of the wisdom and Hokhmah of god, of world-wrenching apocalyptic, of theodicy and evil in the world, there were those who finally drew gnostic conclusions? We know the names of some of these creative Jewish people: John the baptizer, who initiated Jesus of Nazareth and preached apocalyptic ideas in the vicinity of Qumran, where Covenanters and Essenes practiced their separatist, ethical dualism; Simon Magus and Dositheos, who lived about the same time as Jesus and advocated their ideas in Samaria and beyond; Philo of Alexandria, a Hellenistic Jewish thinker who provided Greek philosophical perspectives on the

Hebrew Bible; Rabbi Elisha ben Abuya, nicknamed Aher, "Other," who dabbled in dualism; and there were more. We shall encounter some of these Jewish thinkers in this book. John the baptizer becomes the gnostic hero of the Mandaeans, Jesus of the Christian gnostics. Others, mostly unnamed, may have made similar contributions to the discussion of the profound question of the transcendent god and the demiurge.

The role of the gnostic savior or revealer is to awaken people who are under the spell of the demiurge—not, as in the case of the Christ of the emerging orthodox church, to die for the salvation of people, to be a sacrifice for sins, or to rise from the dead on Easter. The gnostic revealer discloses knowledge that frees and awakens people, and that helps them recall who they are. When enlightened, gnostics can live a life appropriate for those who know themselves and god. They can return back to the beginning, when they were one with god. Such a life transcends what is mundane and mortal in this world and experiences the bliss of oneness with the divine. As the divine forethought, or Christ, in the Secret Book of John says to a person—every person—in the pit of the underworld, "I am the forethought of pure light, I am the thought of the virgin spirit, who raises you to a place of honor. Arise, remember that you have heard, and trace your root, which is I, the compassionate."

Gnostic Wisdom and Knowledge

Gnostic literature includes a typical cast of spiritual or mythological figures and realms, but they are referred to by different names.

Above and beyond all is the transcendent deity. In the Book of Baruch this deity is called the Good and is identified with the fertility god Priapos. In the Secret Book of John and elsewhere this deity is called the One, or monad, as well as the invisible spirit, virgin spirit, and father. It is said that the One should not be confused with a god, since it is greater than a god. Elsewhere the transcendent is called the boundless, depth, majesty, light. Poimandres reveals itself as the light, mind, first god. Mandaeans call this deity the great life and lord of greatness, Manichaeans the father of greatness, Muslim mystics the exalted king, Cathars the invisible father, true god, good god.

The glory of the transcendent is made manifest in a heavenly world of light. In the classic literature of gnostic wisdom, this exalted world is often called the *pleroma* or fullness of god, and the inhabitants of this world are called aeons or eternal realms. The first of the aeons is usually the divine mother. For Simon Magus she is Helena, or *ennoia*, the thought of god. In the Secret Book of John she is Barbelo, or *pronoia*, the first thought or forethought of god. Thunder, in the text by that name, has certain similarities as well. Sometimes the transcendent father and the divine mother produce a child in spiritual love. Often the aeons are identified as spiritual attributes of the divine, are given names, and are joined together as couples, spiritual lovers in the fullness of the divine. In the Mandaean divine world the great life is surrounded by other lives and a host of Jordans, or heavenly waters; in the Manichaean kingdom of light the father of greatness is surrounded by 12 aeons and 144 aeons of aeons; and in the Mother of Books the exalted king is surrounded by seas, angels, lights, and colors.

Among the aeons and manifestations of the divine is often a figure who represents the divine in this world, fallen from the light above yet present as the light of god with us and in us. In many gnostic texts this is the figure called Sophia, or wisdom, as mentioned above. In Valentinian traditions two forms of wisdom are evident, a higher wisdom called Sophia and a lower wisdom called Achamoth. Wisdom is closely linked to Eve in the creation stories, and Eve is portrayed as the mother of the living and a revealer of knowledge. Wisdom may also be linked to the gnostic revealer, and wisdom may take part in the process of salvation. In other texts the divine logos, or word, plays a similar role. Such is also the case with Ruha, the spirit, in Mandaean texts, and perhaps Salman, including great Salman and lesser Salman, in the Islamic Mother of Books. In the Gospel of Judas, the figure of Judas Iscariot seems to assume many of the features of Sophia, or wisdom.

As noted, the demiurge or creator of this world is commonly distinguished from the transcendent deity in gnostic texts. The demiurge is ignorant, tragic, megalomaniacal. In the Secret Book of John he is depicted as the ugly child of Sophia, snakelike in appearance, with the face of a lion and eyes flashing like bolts of lightning. He is named Yaldabaoth, Sakla, Samael, and he is the chief archon and an arrogant, jealous god. In the Gospel of Judas he is given another name, Nebro, said to mean "rebel." In the Gospel of Truth error behaves like the demiurge, for it becomes strong and works in the world, but erroneously. Similar, too, are the actions of Ptahil in Mandaean literature, the five evil archons in Manichaean literature, Azazi'il in the Mother of Books, and Lucifer or Satan among the Cathars.

The gnostic revealer awakens people who are under the spell of the demiurge. Within a Jewish context the gnostic revealer is Seth, the child of Adam and Eve, or the first thought or the insight or the wisdom of the divine. Within a Christian context, the revealer is Jesus the anointed, within a Manichaean context, Jesus of light, as well as others. More abstractly, the call to revelation and knowledge—the wake-up call—is a winged divine messenger in the Song of the Pearl, instruction of mind in Hermetic literature, and enlightened Manda dHayye, knowledge of life, in Mandaean literature. In other words, the call to knowledge is the dawning of awareness, from within and without, of "what is, what was, and what is to come." It is insight. It is gnosis.

In gnostic literature those who come to knowledge are described in different ways. Occasionally they are specifically called gnostics; the Mandaeans are also called by the word that means "gnostics" in Mandaic. More often they are named the unshakable race, or the seed or offspring of Seth, or the generation without a king, or the elect or chosen, or, in the Mother of Books, the ones who know. With a mystical flourish the Gospel of Philip recommends that rather than be called a Christian, a person with knowledge might be understood to be at one with the gnostic revealer and be called Christ. This recalls the Gospel of Thomas, saying 108, where Jesus says, "Whoever drinks from my mouth will become like me. I myself shall become that person, and the hidden things will be revealed to that one." Such people of knowledge know how to live profoundly and well in the truth and light of god. The Gospel of Truth concludes, "It is they who manifest themselves truly, since they are in that true and eternal life and speak of the perfect light filled with the seed of the father, which is in his heart and in the fullness, while his spirit rejoices in it and glorifies him in whom it was, because the father is good. And his children are perfect and worthy of his name, because he is the father. Children like this the father loves."

Gnostic Scriptures

The sacred texts or scriptures presented in this book all help to clarify what gnostic religion is and who the gnostics were. These texts are essential gnostic masterpieces selected from a much larger body of gnostic literary creations that may be included in a "Gnostic Bible."[2] The similarities and differences among these texts are equally instructive, as are the connections among them, whether historical or phenomenological. The early "wisdom gospel" of Thomas, perhaps dating from the first century c.e., portrays Jesus as a speaker of wise words, and it communicates an incipient gnostic perspective. The classic literature of gnostic wisdom dates from the second century c.e., and some materials in the literature are probably even older. Justin's Book of Baruch illustrates a Jewish form of gnostic spirituality with Greco-Roman allusions. So does Sethian gnostic literature, with its provocative Jewish interpretation of the opening chapters of Genesis and its emphasis on the special roles of Eve, the mother of the living, and Seth, whom the Sethian gnostics claimed as ancestor. Valentinian gnostic literature is named after the great second-century teacher Valentinos, who, along with his students, seems to have made use of Sethian insights in order to fashion an elegant gnostic system for reflecting upon the origin and destiny of true life and light. In

Syria, the sacred literature relating to Thomas is closely related to the wisdom gospel of Thomas; Thomas is understood to be the twin of Jesus and the guarantor of his wisdom and knowledge.

The Hermetic literature dates from the first century c.e. and after. It is named after the Greek god Hermes, the divine messenger, nicknamed Trismegistos, "thrice-greatest," and depicted in a syncretistic way, once again with Jewish and Greco-Roman themes, along with Egyptian motifs. The Mandaeans consist of Middle Eastern gnostic communities that exist to the present day, now in locales around the world. The Mandaeans interpret the opening chapters of Genesis in a typically gnostic manner, but they reserve a special place for John the baptizer, whose style of Jewish baptismal piety they considered to reflect the origin of their communities. Manichaean literature dates from the time of Mani, the third-century prophet who, with his followers, created a world religion intended to be universal. Manichaeism draws from Zoroastrian, Buddhist, and Christian sources, likely including the Gospel of Thomas and other gnostic texts, in order to announce how the divine light of the cosmos may be saved from the machinations of the forces of darkness and gathered into the kingdom of light. Some of the songs in the Coptic Manichaean Songbook appear to be related to Mandaean literature, and Manichaeism and Mandaeism show connections with each other.

Such Islamic mystical texts as the Mother of Books, as well as Cathar sacred literature, are sometimes described by scholars as late gnostic or Neomanichaean, because of similarities with the traditions of Mani and his followers. The Mother of Books comes from the eighth century c.e. and represents a form of Islamic *ghuluw*, which literally means "exaggeration." The Cathar texts come from medieval Europe and offer a dualistic message of the triumph of light over darkness. The Cathars, like so many gnostics, venerated the Gospel of John. The Gospel of the Secret Supper features John and cites a portion of the Gospel of John as it announces the glory that will finally come to the children of the good god of light: "The just will glow like a sun in the kingdom of the invisible father. And the son of god will take them before the throne of the invisible father and say to them, 'Here I am with my children whom you have given me. Just father, the world has not known you, but I have truly known you, because it is you who have sent me on my mission.'"

What Is Gnosis?

In assembling *The Essential Gnostics,* what definitions have we used? Where have we drawn the line? Let us examine our definitions more carefully.

The term *gnostic* is derived from the ancient Greek word *gnosis,* "knowledge." *Gnosis* is a common word in Greek, and it can designate different types of knowledge. Sometimes, as in the sacred texts included in this book, gnosis means "personal or mystical knowledge." Understood in this way, gnosis may mean "acquaintance," that is, knowledge as personal awareness of oneself or another person or even god, or it may mean "insight," that is, knowledge as immediate awareness of deep truths. These ways of understanding gnosis are not mutually exclusive, for knowledge may entail the immediate awareness of oneself or of another, in a personal union or communion that provides profound insight into the true nature of everything. As we have already noted, the Gospel of Thomas has Jesus articulate just such a mystical personal knowledge.

The gnosis sought by the authors of these texts is hardly ordinary knowledge. A text from the Nag Hammadi library, the Exegesis on the Soul, declares that the restoration of the soul to a state of wholeness "is not due to rote phrases or to professional skills or to book learning." Indeed, mystics commonly have emphasized, in many books, that mystical knowledge cannot be attained simply by reading books. Other texts describe this sort of gnosis by listing questions that need to be addressed if one is to be enlightened by knowledge. In the Secret Book of John, the savior or revealer announces that she or he will

teach "what is, what was, and what is to come," and in the Book of
Thomas the revealer commands, "Examine yourself and understand
who you are, how you exist, and how you will come to be." To attain
this knowledge—to become a gnostic—is to know oneself, god, and
everything. Or, in the words of the maxim from the ancient oracular
center dedicated to Apollo at Delphi, Greece, a maxim cited frequently
in the texts discussed here: *gnothi sauton*, "know yourself." According
to many of these sacred texts, to know oneself truly is to attain this
mystical knowledge, and to attain this mystical knowledge is to
know oneself truly. Gnostic knowledge, then, relies on lived mystical
experience, on knowledge of the whole time line of the world, past,
present, and future, and on knowledge of the self—where we have
come from, who we are, where we are going—and of the soul's
journey.

Thus, the Greek word *gnosis* was used extensively by people in
the world of Mediterranean antiquity, including the people who
wrote the texts presented in this book, but among the heresiologists
the word was employed in a particularly polemical fashion. The
heresiologists were heresy hunters who, as the guardians of truth and
watchmen on the walls of Zion, were trying to expose people judged
to be dangerous to the masses, especially the Christian masses. The
more famous of the heresiologists include Irenaeus of Lyon, whose
major work was *Adversus haereses*, "Against Heresies"; Hippolytus
of Rome, who wrote *Refutatio omnium haeresium*, "Refutation of
All Heresies"; Pseudo-Tertullian (an author writing under the name
of Tertullian), who wrote *Adversus omnes haereses*, "Against All
Heresies"; and Epiphanius of Salamis, who authored a particularly
nasty piece entitled *Panarion*, "Medicine Chest," with an orthodox
remedy for every heretical malady. The Neoplatonist philosopher
Plotinos of Lykopolis also wrote a heresiological treatise, *Against the
Gnostics*, according to his student Porphyry. All these heresiologists
focused, to one extent or another, upon the supposed gnosis of
the heretics, and they suggested that at least some—even if only a
few—of the heretics could be called *gnostikoi*, gnostics, or referred

to themselves as *gnostikoi*. While these heretics used the word *gnosis*, they did not all necessarily call themselves gnostics. Irenaeus wrote five volumes against heresies, and he claimed to have composed an "exposé and refutation of falsely so-called knowledge." Irenaeus and his fellow heresiologists, motivated by a religious zeal to expose and refute people with whom they disagreed, were rather sloppy and imprecise in their use of terms and their enumeration of heresies. Yet their presentations of gnosis, "falsely so-called gnosis," have played a role, albeit a polemical one, in defining the terms *gnosis*, *gnostic*, and *gnosticism* in modern discussions.

The widespread use of the word *gnosis* (and similar words in other languages, for example, in Coptic and Latin), and the polemical application of this word and related words among the heresiologists, have created a challenge for scholars and students who wish to understand gnostic religion. What is the religion of gnosis? *Gnosis* is a word widely attested in the ancient world, but the word *gnosticism* itself is a term not attested at all in antiquity or late antiquity. Rather, it was first used in the eighteenth century to designate the heretical religious groups discussed by the heresiologists. Are "gnosticism" and "gnosis" valid categories for analysis? Who actually were the gnostics? These questions have become even more interesting when scholars have reflected upon gnosis in relation to Hermetic, Mandaean, Manichaean, Shi'ite, and Cathar religions. Further, the discovery and publication in recent times of primary texts (as opposed to the secondary texts of the heresiologists) generally considered to be gnostic has raised the issues of definition and taxonomy in new and exciting ways. Among these primary texts are those from the Askew Codex (Pistis Sophia, or Faith Wisdom), the Bruce Codex, the Berlin Gnostic Codex 8502, the Nag Hammadi library, and Codex Tchacos. The Nag Hammadi library is a treasure trove of Coptic texts, most previously unknown and many considered gnostic by scholars. The texts in the Nag Hammadi library were discovered around December 1945 near Nag Hammadi in upper Egypt, and they are now becoming available in editions and translations. A substantial number of texts in the present book are from the Nag Hammadi library. One text, the Gospel of Judas, is from the recently published Codex Tchacos.[3]

What Are Scriptures? What Is a Bible?

The texts in this collection are classics of sacred literature, and we present them as gnostic scriptures in what might be termed a "Gnostic Bible." The term *Bible* is derived ultimately from the ancient Greek word *biblos* (or *bublos*), meaning "papyrus," the reed used to make a primitive sort of paper in order to construct scrolls and codices, or books, in the world of ancient bookbinding. The Greek word was also written in a diminutive form, *biblion*; the plural is *biblia*, "books." Within the context of Judaism and Christianity certain books came to be associated with the sacred scriptures, which in turn were eventually referred to in the singular, the Bible. Thus, within the history of the use of the term, the Bible, or the book, designates a collection or anthology of sacred texts.

We can explain how this set of meanings came to be associated with the word *Bible* by examining the process of establishing a canon or canons within Judaism and Christianity. Organized religions usually teach that adherents to a given religion should observe the tenets of the tradition in a way that is right, proper, and correct according to a given canon. (Originally a canon was a cane or reed, a measuring stick, but the term came to be applied to any standard by which one might determine whether a person's thoughts or actions measure up to the standard of correctness in the tradition.) Judaism, Christianity, and Islam are religions of the book, and so their canons are written canons, authoritative books and anthologies. For Judaism and Christianity, the authoritative books are the Jewish Bible (or, more exactly, the Tanakh, that is, the Torah ["law"], Neviim ["prophets"], and Kethuvim ["writings"]) and the New Testament (or the New Covenant), respectively. The Jewish Bible was used in antiquity in Hebrew and in Greek translation. The Greek version, called the Septuagint, was completed in Alexandria, Egypt, by bilingual Jewish translators during the first centuries B.C.E. for Greek-speaking Jews who could no longer read the Hebrew texts with ease. A legend emerged that the Septuagint was written in a miraculously identical fashion by seventy-two translators who labored in pairs over a period of seventy-two days. The Septuagint was the Bible of the early Christian church, which originated, after all, as a Jewish religious movement. This Greek translation of the scriptures of Judaism contains several texts not included in the Hebrew Bible—for example, Baruch, 1 Esdras, Judith, 1–4 Maccabees, Sirach, Tobit, and the Wisdom of Solomon. To this day the inclusion or exclusion of these texts contained in the Septuagint remains a canonical issue among Protestant, Roman Catholic, and Orthodox Christians.

The formation of the New Testament as the Christian Bible was a gradual process that took centuries to complete. Finally, at the Council of Trent in 1545, the Roman Catholic Church acted to recognize its list of biblical, canonical books as final, that is, closed to any additions or subtractions. (Minor changes from the work of textual critics are quietly incorporated into new printings of Bible translations.) Many Protestant denominations have never acted officially to recognize a biblical canon. While there is widespread agreement among Christians concerning what books should be included in the New Testament, the traditions of the Syrian and Ethiopic churches have claimed that different sets of texts should be included in the Christian canon. Today some are proposing the Gospel of Thomas as an authoritative Christian text, and the Jesus Seminar in Santa Rosa, California, has discussed the possibility of a new New Testament, a new Christian Bible. *The Restored New Testament* by Willis Barnstone goes further, including the Gospels of Thomas, Mary, and Judas as translated by Barnstone and Meyer.

Arguably the most influential person in the process of the formation of a New Testament was a second-century Christian teacher, a dyed-in-the-wool dualist named Marcion of Sinope. Marcion is sometimes included in discussions of the gnostics because of his radical dualism, but his Christian religion was a religion of faith rather than gnosis. We consider Marcion to be an unrepentant Paulinist, with a literalistic way of reading the Bible rather than a gnostic way. As one prominent scholar quipped, the only person in the second century who understood Paul was Marcion, and he misunderstood him.

Marcion was a rich shipowner turned evangelist who went to Rome in the middle of the second century in order to contribute his money and his teachings to the Roman church. Both were returned to him. Marcion preached that the good and loving god, revealed in Christ, must be distinguished from the just and righteous god, who was the god of the Jewish people. Marcion's theological dualism, with all its anti-Semitic implications, necessitated for him the creation of a new Bible, a new authoritative book for the god newly revealed in Christ. Marcion wrote a book, a rather simpleminded piece called the *Antitheses*, with quotations from Jewish and Christian texts that seemed to Marcion to show the striking contrasts between the Jewish god and the Christian god. Marcion also formulated a Christian canon—as far as we can tell, he was the first Christian to come up with the idea of a separate Christian Bible. He knew of a series of letters of Paul, and he knew of the Gospel of Luke, which he considered Paul's gospel, and he combined these into his New Testament. And when he read in Paul's letter to the Galatians that some troublesome people want to "pervert the gospel of Christ" (1:7), he took the words seriously and literally. He assumed that lackeys of the Jewish god were perverting the written texts by penning in words favorable to the Jewish god and the scriptures of the Jewish god. Marcion responded as a highly opinionated textual critic by removing the sections of Paul's letters and Luke's gospel that he thought needed to be erased in order to restore the texts to their original form. For Marcion's misguided efforts his foe Tertullian chided him, "Shame on Marcion's eraser!"

Marcion proved to be popular and influential as a leader of his church, but only for a time. Eventually he was rejected by many Christians, including the heresiologists, and declared a heretic. The

Christians opposed to Marcion disliked his insistence on two gods and his rejection of Judaism and the god of the Hebrew Bible. Instead, such Christians looked for continuity in the history of salvation from Judaism to Jesus and beyond. Yet the Christian canonical idea of Marcion carried the day, as did Marcion's basic outline of the Christian canon, with a gospel section and an epistolary (Pauline) section. From the perspective of the Christian Bible, Marcion lost the battle but won the war.

When we refer to the texts in the present book as scriptures of gnosis, we are in this world of discourse. We are presenting these texts as sacred books and sacred scriptures of the gnostics, and collectively as sacred literature of the gnostics. But in this Bible of the gnostics there is no sense of a single, authoritative collection. The sacred literature in this Bible illustrates a diversity that we have suggested is characteristic of gnostic religions. Further, the sacred literature in this Bible constitutes no closed canon. We present here what we judge to be among the most significant and compelling gnostic texts, and there are many other gnostic texts that have not been included. All these gnostic texts may be equally authoritative, truths may be discovered in a variety of texts and traditions, and the way to wisdom and knowledge cannot be closed. Such a sense of wisdom and knowledge has made this sacred literature attractive to free spirits in the past and equally fascinating to many in the present day.

The Translations

The English translations presented here include some of the most stirring selections of sacred gnostic literature that have survived from antiquity, late antiquity, and the medieval period. These contributions are based on our previous volume, *The Gnostic Bible,* and on the audiobook with the same title. The translations have been updated and revised, and as in the second edition of *The Gnostic Bible,* the Gospel of Judas has been added to the collection. (It has been possible to include new papyrus fragments in the translation of the Gospel of Judas.) Some of the texts are given in the entirety of what has survived of the original documents (for instance, the Gospels of Thomas, Mary, and Judas), some are presented with representative portions of the texts (for example, the Secret Books of John and James and the Gospels of Philip and Truth). For a goodly number of the texts, we offer them in English as poetry, in keeping with the poetic nuances of the original works in their original languages. There are occasional lacunae, or gaps, in some of the texts (for example, the Gospels of Mary and Judas, and Thunder), and these lacunae are indicated by an appropriate amount of blank space left on the pages of this book, in order to approximate the actual appearance of the original manuscript. In the cases of the texts that derive from earlier periods of time, we employ Semitic forms of the names of people and places, since these texts reflect more nearly the Semitic world of Jesus—or, rather, Yeshua—and his disciples or students, a world in which Hebrew and Aramaic rather than Greek and Latin were often preferred languages. Such Semitic forms within the translations may also provide a fresh approach to these earlier texts by suggesting an eastern Mediterranean orientation for many of the themes and motifs found on their ancient pages. There are relatively few explanatory notes in this edition, and the introductions are very brief. For a fuller discussion of the interpretation of these texts, the reader is referred to *The Gnostic Bible*.

1

THE GOSPEL
OF THOMAS

THE GOSPEL OF THOMAS is the opening text in this collection of sacred texts of knowledge and wisdom.[1] Unlike the New Testament gospels, which emphasize the cross and resurrection of Jesus, the Gospel of Thomas is a gospel of wisdom. The value of Jesus in the Gospel of Thomas lies in his wise sayings, which communicate life and salvation. According to this gospel, those who follow Jesus, respond to his words, and find the meaning of what Jesus says, discover true life.

The Gospel of Thomas has traditionally been divided by scholars into 114 sayings, and that convention is also followed here. The translations are based on the Coptic version of the Gospel of Thomas from the Nag Hammadi library. Within the sayings the original forms of the Semitic names of characters are given. Thus, Yeshua is the name used for Jesus, Yehuda Toma for Judas Thomas, Yaakov for James, Shimon Kefa for Simon Peter, Matai for Matthew, Miryam for Mary, and Yohanan for John. Shabbat is the Sabbath, and Yehuda is the land of Judea.

～

These are the hidden sayings that the living Yeshua spoke and Yehuda Toma the twin recorded.

(1) And he said,
     Whoever discovers what these sayings mean
     will not taste death.

(2) Yeshua says,
     Seek and do not stop seeking until you find.
     When you find, you will be troubled.
     When you are troubled,
     you will marvel and rule over all.[2]

(3) Yeshua says,
     If your leaders tell you, "Look, the kingdom is in heaven,"
     then the birds of heaven will precede you.
     If they say to you, "It's in the sea,"[3]
     then the fish will precede you.
     But the kingdom is inside you and it is outside you.
     When you know yourselves, then you will be known,
     and you will understand that you are children of the living
          father.
     But if you do not know yourselves,
     then you dwell in poverty and you are poverty.

(4) Yeshua says,
     A person old in days
     will not hesitate to ask a little child
     seven days old about the place of life,
     and the person will live.
     For many of the first will be last
     and become a single one.

(5) Yeshua says,
   Know what is in front of your face
   and what is hidden from you will be disclosed.
   There is nothing hidden that will not be revealed.[4]

(6) His students asked him and said to him,
   Do you want us to fast?
   How should we pray?
   Should we give to charity?
   What diet should we observe?

   Yeshua says,
   Do not lie and do not do what you hate.
   All things are disclosed before heaven.
   There is nothing hidden that will not be revealed,
   nothing covered that will remain undisclosed.

(7) Yeshua says,
   Blessings on the lion if a human eats it,
   making the lion human.
   Foul is the human if a lion eats it,
   making the lion human.

(8) And he says,
   Humankind is like a wise fisherman who cast his net
       into the sea
   and drew it up from the sea full of little fish.
   Among the fish he found a fine large fish.
   He threw all the little fish back into the sea
   and easily chose the large fish.
   Whoever has ears to hear should hear.

(9) Yeshua says,
   Look, the sower went out, took a handful of seeds,
   and scattered them.
   Some fell on the road
   and the birds came and pecked them up.
   Others fell on rock
   and they did not take root in the soil
   and did not produce heads of grain.
   Others fell on thorns
   and they choked the seeds
   and worms devoured them.
   And others fell on good soil
   and it brought forth a good crop,
   yielding sixty per measure and one hundred twenty
      per measure.

(10) Yeshua says,
   I have thrown fire upon the world,
   and look, I am watching till it blazes.

(11) Yeshua says,
   This heaven will pass away
   and the one above it will pass away.
   The dead are not alive
   and the living will not die.
   During the days when you ate what is dead
   you made it alive.
   When you are in the light, what will you do?
   On the day when you were one
   you became two.
   But when you become two, what will you do?

(12) The students said to Yeshua,
      We know you will leave us.
      Who will be our leader?

      Yeshua said to them,
      Wherever you are, seek out Yaakov the just.
      For his sake heaven and earth came into being.

(13) Yeshua said to his students,
      Compare me to something
      and tell me what I am like.

      Shimon Kefa said to him,
      You are like a just messenger.

      Matai said to him,
      You are like a wise philosopher.

      Toma said to him,
      Rabbi,[5] my mouth is utterly unable to say
      what you are like.

      Yeshua said,
      I am not your rabbi.
      Because you have drunk, you are intoxicated
      from the bubbling spring I tended.

      And he took him and withdrew, and spoke three sayings
          to him.

      When Toma came back to his friends, they asked him,
      What did Yeshua say to you?

Toma said to them,
If I tell you one of the sayings he spoke to me,
you will pick up rocks and stone me
and fire will come out of the rocks and consume you.

(14) Yeshua says to them,
If you fast you will bring sin upon yourselves,
and if you pray you will be condemned,
and if you give to charity you will harm your spirits.
When you go into any region and walk through the
countryside,
and people receive you, eat what they serve you
and heal the sick among them.
What goes into your mouth will not defile you,
but what comes out of your mouth will defile you.

(15) Yeshua says,
When you see one not born of woman,
fall on your faces and worship.
That is your father.

(16) Yeshua says,
People may think I have come to impose peace upon the
world.
They do not know that I have come to impose conflicts upon
the earth: fire, sword, war.
For there will be five in a house.
There will be three against two and two against three,
father against son and son against father,
and they will stand alone.

(17) Yeshua says,
> I shall give you what no eye has seen, what no ear has heard,
> what no hand has touched, what has not arisen in the human
> heart.

(18) The students said to Yeshua,
> Tell us how our end will be.

> Yeshua says,
> Have you discovered the beginning and now are seeking
> the end?
> Where the beginning is, the end will be.
> Blessings on you who stand at the beginning.
> You will know the end and not taste death.

(19) Yeshua says,
> Blessings on you who came into being
> before coming into being.
> If you become my students and hear my sayings,
> these stones will serve you.
> For there are five trees in paradise for you.
> Summer or winter they do not change
> and their leaves do not fall.
> Whoever knows them will not taste death.

(20) The students said to Yeshua,
> Tell us what the kingdom of heaven is like.

> He says to them,
> It is like a mustard seed, the tiniest of seeds,
> but when it falls on prepared soil,

it produces a great plant
and becomes a shelter for the birds of heaven.

(21) Miryam said to Yeshua,
What are your students like?

He says,
They are like children living in a field that is not theirs.
When the owners of the field come, they will say,
"Give our field back to us."
The children take off their clothes in front of them
to give it back,
and they return their field to them.
So I say, if the owner of a house knows that a thief is coming,
he will be on guard before the thief arrives
and will not let the thief break into the house of his estate
and steal his possessions.
As for you, be on guard against the world.
Arm yourselves with great strength,
or the robbers will find a way to reach you,
for the trouble you expect will come.
Let someone among you understand.
When the crop ripened,
the reaper came quickly with sickle in hand
and harvested it.
Whoever has ears to hear should hear.

(22) Yeshua saw some babies nursing. He said to his students,
These nursing babies
are like those who enter the kingdom.

They said to him,
Then shall we enter the kingdom as babies?

Yeshua says to them,
When you make the two into one,
and when you make the inner like the outer
and the outer like the inner
and the upper like the lower,
and when you make male and female into a single one,
so that the male will not be male nor the female be female,
when you make eyes in place of an eye,
a hand in place of a hand,
a foot in place of a foot,
an image in place of an image,
then you will enter the kingdom.

(23) Yeshua says,
I shall choose you as one from a thousand
and as two from ten thousand
and they will stand as a single one.

(24) His students said,
Show us the place where you are.
We must seek it.

He says to them,
Whoever has ears should hear.
There is light within a person of light
and it shines on the whole world.
If it does not shine it is dark.

(25) Yeshua says,
      Love your brother like your soul.
      Protect that person like the pupil of your eye.

(26) Yeshua says,
      You see the speck in your brother's eye
      but not the beam in your own eye.
      When you take the beam out of your own eye,
      then you will see clearly to take the speck out of your
            brother's eye.

(27) If you do not fast from the world, you will not find the
            kingdom.
      If you do not observe the Shabbat as Shabbat,
      you will not see the father.

(28) Yeshua says,
      I took my stand in the midst of the world,
      and I appeared to them in flesh.
      I found them all drunk
      yet none of them thirsty.
      My soul ached for the human children
      because they are blind in their hearts
      and do not see.
      They came into the world empty
      and seek to depart from the world empty.
      But now they are drunk.
      When they shake off their wine, they will repent.

(29) Yeshua says,
> If the flesh came into being because of spirit,
> it is a marvel,
> but if spirit came into being because of body,
> it is a marvel of marvels.
> Yet I marvel at how this great wealth has come to dwell
> in this poverty.

(30) Yeshua says,
> Where there are three deities,
> they are divine.
> Where there are two or one,
> I am with that one.[6]

(31) Yeshua says,
> A prophet is not accepted in the hometown.
> A doctor does not heal those who know the doctor.

(32) Yeshua says,
> A city built upon a high hill and fortified cannot fall,
> nor can it be hidden.

(33) Yeshua says,
> What you will hear in your ear
> in the other ear[7] proclaim from your rooftops.
> No one lights a lamp and puts it under a basket,
> nor in a hidden place.
> You put it on a stand
> so that all who come and go will see its light.

(34) Yeshua says,
If a blind person leads a blind person,
both will fall in a hole.

(35) Yeshua says,
You cannot enter the house of the strong
and take it by force without binding the owner's hands.
Then you can loot the house.

(36) Yeshua says,
From morning to evening and from evening to morning,
do not worry about what you will wear.[8]

(37) His students said,
When will you appear to us
and when shall we see you?

Yeshua says,
When you strip naked without being ashamed
and take your clothes and put them under your feet
like small children and trample them,
then you will see the child of the living one
and you will not be afraid.

(38) Yeshua says,
Often you wanted to hear these sayings I am telling you,
and you have no one else from whom to hear them.
There will be days when you will seek me
and you will not find me.

(39) Yeshua says,
> The Pharisees and the scholars have taken the keys of
> knowledge
> and have hidden them.
> They have not entered,
> nor have they allowed those who want to enter
> to go inside.
> You should be shrewd as snakes and innocent as doves.

(40) Yeshua says,
> A grapevine has been planted far from the father.
> Since it is not strong
> it will be pulled up by the root and perish.

(41) Yeshua says,
> Whoever has something in hand will be given more
> and whoever has nothing will be deprived
> of the paltry things possessed.

(42) Yeshua says,
> Be passersby.

(43) His students said to him,
> Who are you to say these things to us?

> Yeshua says,
> From what I tell you, you do not know
> who I am,
> but you have become like the Jews.

They love the tree but hate its fruit
or love the fruit but hate the tree.

(44) Yeshua says,
Whoever blasphemes against the father
will be forgiven,
and whoever blasphemes against the son
will be forgiven,
but whoever blasphemes against the holy spirit will not be
    forgiven,
either on earth or in heaven.

(45) Yeshua says,
Grapes are not harvested from thorn trees,
nor are figs gathered from thistles.
They yield no fruit.
A good person brings forth good from the storehouse.
A bad person brings forth evil things
from the corrupt storehouse in the heart
and says evil things.
From the abundance of the heart
such a person brings forth evil.

(46) Yeshua says,
From Adam to Yohanan the baptizer,
among those born of women,
no one of you is so much greater than Yohanan
that your eyes should not be averted.
But I have said that whoever among you becomes a child
will know the kingdom
and become greater than Yohanan.

(47) Yeshua says,

A person cannot mount two horses or bend two bows,
and a servant cannot serve two masters,
or the servant will honor one and offend the other.
No one who drinks aged wine
suddenly wants to drink new wine.
New wine is not poured into aged wineskins
or they may break,
and aged wine is not poured into a new wineskin
or it may spoil.
An old patch is not sewn onto a new garment
or it may tear.

(48) Yeshua says,

If two make peace with each other in one house,
they will tell the mountain, "Move,"
and the mountain will move.

(49) Yeshua says,

Blessings on you who are alone and chosen,
for you will find the kingdom.
You have come from it
and will return there again.

(50) Yeshua says,

If they say to you, "Where have you come from?"
say to them, "We have come from the light,
from the place where the light came into being by itself,
established itself, and appeared in their image."
If they say to you, "Is it you?"
say, "We are its children and the chosen of the living father."

If they ask you, "What is the evidence of your father in you?"
say to them, "It is motion and rest."

(51) His students said to him,
When will the dead rest?
When will the new world come?

He says to them,
What you look for has come
but you do not know it.

(52) His students said to him,
Twenty-four prophets have spoken in Israel
and they all spoke of you.

He says to them,
You have disregarded the living one among you
and have spoken of the dead.

(53) His students said to him,
Is circumcision useful or not?

He says to them,
If it were useful, fathers would produce their children
already circumcised from their mothers.
But the true circumcision in spirit
is altogether valuable.

(54) Yeshua says,
Blessings on you the poor,
for yours is the kingdom of heaven.

(55) Yeshua says,
Those who do not hate their father and mother
cannot be my students,
and those who do not hate their brothers and sisters
and bear the cross as I do
will not be worthy of me.

(56) Yeshua says,
Whoever has come to know the world
has discovered a carcass,
and whoever has discovered a carcass,
of that person the world is not worthy.

(57) Yeshua says,
The father's kingdom is like someone with good seed.
His enemy came at night and sowed weeds among the
    good seed.
He did not let them pull up the weeds
but said to them,
"No, or you might go to pull up the weeds
and pull up the wheat along with them."
On harvest day the weeds will be conspicuous
and will be pulled up and burned.

(58) Yeshua says,
Blessings on the person who has labored[9]
and found life.

(59) Yeshua says,
Look to the living one as long as you live
or you may die and try to see the living one
and you will not be able to see.

(60) He saw a Samaritan carrying a lamb as he was going to the
land of Yehuda.

He said to his students,
That person is carrying
the lamb around.[10]

They said to him,
Then he may kill it
and eat it.

He said to them,
He will not eat it while it is alive
but only after he has killed it
and it has become a carcass.

They said,
Otherwise he cannot do it.

He says to them,
So with you. Seek a place of rest
or you may become a carcass and be eaten.

(61) Yeshua says,
Two will rest on a couch. One will die, one will live.

Salome said,
Who are you, mister? You have climbed on my couch
and eaten from my table as if you are from someone.

Yeshua said to her,
I am the one who comes from what is whole.
I was given from the things of my father.

Salome said,
I am your student.

Yeshua says,
I say, if you are whole, you will be filled with light,
but if divided, you will be filled with darkness.

(62) Yeshua says,
I disclose my mysteries to those who are worthy
of my mysteries.
Do not let your left hand know
what your right hand is doing.

(63) Yeshua says,
There was a rich person who was very wealthy.
He said, "I shall invest my money so I may sow, reap, plant,
and fill my storehouses with produce.
Then I shall lack nothing."
This is what he was thinking in his heart,
but that very night he died.
Whoever has ears should hear.

(64) Yeshua says,
      A person was receiving guests. When he prepared the dinner
      he sent his servant to invite the guests.
      The servant went to the first and said,
      "My master invites you."

      That person said,
      "Some merchants owe me money.
      They are coming tonight.
      I must go and give them instructions.
      Please excuse me from dinner."

      The servant went to another and said,
      "My master invites you."

      He said to the servant,
      "I have bought a house
      and I've been called away for a day.
      I have no time."

      The servant went to another and said,
      "My master invites you."

      He said to the servant,
      "My friend is to be married
      and I am to arrange the banquet.
      I can't come. Please excuse me from dinner."

      The servant went to another and said,
      "My master invites you."

      He said to the servant,
      "I have bought an estate
      and I am going to collect rent.

I shall not be able to come. Please excuse me."

The servant returned and said to his master,
"Those you invited to dinner have asked to be excused."

The master said to his servant,
"Go out into the streets and invite whomever you find for the
    dinner."
Buyers and merchants will not enter the places of my father.

(65) He says,
A usurer[11] owned a vineyard and rented it
to some farmers to work it
and from them he would collect its produce.
He sent his servant for the farmers to give him
the produce of the vineyard. They seized, beat,
and almost killed his servant, who returned
and told his master. His master said,
"Perhaps he did not know them." And he sent
another servant, but they beat him as well.
Then the master sent his son and said,
"Perhaps they will respect my son."
Since the farmers knew the son was the heir
of the vineyard, they seized him and killed him.
Whoever has ears should hear.

(66) Yeshua says,
Show me the stone that the builders rejected.
That is the cornerstone.

(67) Yeshua says,
One who knows all but lacks within
is utterly lacking.

(68) Yeshua says,
Blessings on you when you are hated and persecuted,
and no place will be found,
wherever you are persecuted.

(69) Yeshua says,
Blessings on you who have been persecuted in your hearts.
Only you truly know the father.
Blessings on you who are hungry
that the stomach of someone else in want may be filled.

(70) Yeshua says,
If you bring forth what is within you, what you have will
    save you.
If you have nothing within you,
what you do not have within you will kill you.

(71) Yeshua says,
I shall destroy this house
and no one will be able to rebuild it.

(72) Someone said to him,
Tell my brothers to divide my father's possessions with me.

He said to the person,
Mister, who made me a divider?

He turned to his students and said to them,
I am not a divider, am I?

(73) Yeshua says,

> The harvest is large but the workers are few.
> Beg the master to send out workers to the harvest.

(74) He said,[12]

> Master, there are many around the drinking trough
> but nothing in the well.

(75) Yeshua says,

> There are many standing at the door
> but those who are alone will enter the wedding chamber.

(76) Yeshua says,

> The father's kingdom is like a merchant
> who owned a supply of merchandise and found a pearl.
> The merchant was prudent.
> He sold his goods and bought the single pearl
> for himself.
> So with you. Seek his treasure that is unfailing
> and enduring,
> where no moth comes to devour and no worm destroys.

(77) Yeshua says,

> I am the light over all things.
> I am all.
> From me all has come forth,
> and to me all has reached.
> Split a piece of wood.
> I am there.

Lift up the stone
and you will find me there.

(78) Yeshua says,
Why have you come out to the countryside?
To see a reed shaken by the wind?
Or to see a person dressed in soft clothes
like your rulers and your people of power?
They are dressed in soft clothes
and cannot understand truth.

(79) A woman in the crowd said to him,
Blessings on the womb that bore you
and the breasts that fed you.

He says to her,
Blessings on those who have heard the word of the father
and have truly kept it. Days will come when you will say,
"Blessings on the womb that has not conceived
and the breasts that have not given milk."

(80) Yeshua says,
Whoever has come to know the world
has discovered the body,
and whoever has discovered the body,
of that person the world is not worthy.

(81) Yeshua says,
Let a person of wealth rule,
and a person of power renounce it.

(82) Yeshua says,

Whoever is near me is near fire,
and whoever is far from me is far from the kingdom.

(83) Yeshua says,

You see images,
but the light within them is hidden in the image
of the father's light.
He will be disclosed,
but his image is hidden by his light.

(84) Yeshua says,

When you see your likeness you are happy.
But when you see your images that came into being
    before you
and that neither die nor become visible,
how much you will bear!

(85) Yeshua says,

Adam came from great power and great wealth,
but he was not worthy of you.
Had he been worthy,
he would not have tasted death.

(86) Yeshua says,

Foxes have their dens and birds have their nests,
but the human child has no place to lay his head
    and rest.

(87) Yeshua says,
How miserable is the body that depends on a body,
and how miserable is the soul that depends on both.

(88) Yeshua says,
The messengers and the prophets will come to you
and give you what is yours.
You give them what you have and wonder,
"When will they come and take what is theirs?"

(89) Yeshua says,
Why do you wash the outside of the cup?
Don't you understand that the one who made the inside
also made the outside?

(90) Yeshua says,
Come to me, for my yoke is easy and my mastery gentle,
and you will find rest for yourselves.

(91) They said to him,
Tell us who you are so that we may believe in you.

He says to them,
You examine the face of heaven and earth
but you have not come to know the one who is in your
    presence,
and you do not know how to examine this moment.

(92) Yeshua says,
    Seek and you will find.
    In the past I did not tell you the things about which
        you asked me.
    Now I am willing to tell you, but you do not seek them.

(93) Do not give what is holy to dogs.
    They might throw them upon the manure pile.
    Do not throw pearls to swine.
    They might make mud of it.[13]

(94) Yeshua says,
    One who seeks will find.
    For one who knocks it will be opened.

(95) Yeshua says,
    If you have money, do not lend it at interest,
    but give it to someone
    from whom you will not get it back.

(96) Yeshua says,
    The father's kingdom is like a woman
    who took a little yeast, hid it in dough,
    and made large loaves of bread.
    Whoever has ears should hear.

(97) Yeshua says,
    The father's kingdom is like a woman
    who was carrying a jar full of meal.

While she was walking along a distant road,
the handle of the jar broke
and the meal spilled behind her along the road.
She did not know it.
She noticed no problem.
When she reached her house she put the jar down
and found it empty.

(98) Yeshua says,
The father's kingdom is like a person
who wanted to put someone powerful to death.
While at home he drew his sword
and thrust it into the wall
to find out whether his hand would go in.
Then he killed the powerful person.

(99) The students said to him,
Your brothers and your mother are standing outside.

He says to them,
Those here who do the will of my father
are my brothers and my mother.
They will enter my father's kingdom.

(100) They showed Yeshua a gold coin and said to him,
Caesar's people demand taxes from us.

He says to them,
Give Caesar the things that are Caesar's,
give god the things that are god's,
and give me what is mine.

(101) Those who do not hate their father and mother as I do
cannot be my students,
and those who do not love their father and mother as I do
cannot be my students.
For my mother gave me falsehood,[14]
but my true mother gave me life.

(102) Yeshua says,
Shame on the Pharisees.
They are like a dog sleeping in the cattle manger.
It does not eat or let the cattle eat.

(103) Yeshua says,
Blessings on you if you know where the robbers will enter
so you can wake up, rouse your estate,
and arm yourself before they break in.

(104) They said to Yeshua,
Come let us pray today and fast.

Yeshua says,
What sin have I committed
or how have I been undone?
When the bridegroom leaves the wedding chamber,
then let the people fast and pray.

(105) Yeshua says,
Whoever knows the father and the mother
will be called the child of a whore.

(106) Yeshua says,

> When you make two into one,
> you will become human children.
> When you say, "Mountain, move,"
> the mountain will move.

(107) Yeshua says,

> The kingdom is like a shepherd who had
> a hundred sheep.
> One of them, the largest, went astray.
> He left the ninety-nine and looked for the one until he
>   found it.
> After so much trouble he said to the sheep,
> "I love you more than the ninety-nine."

(108) Yeshua says,

> Whoever drinks from my mouth will become like me.
> I myself shall become that person,
> and the hidden things will be revealed to that one.

(109) Yeshua says,

> The kingdom is like a person who had a treasure hidden
>   in his field.
> He did not know it, and when he died, he left it to his son.
> The son did not know about it.
> He took over the field and sold it.
> The buyer was plowing and found the treasure,
> and began to lend money at interest to whomever he wished.

(110) Yeshua says,
You who have found the world
and become wealthy,
renounce the world.

(111) Yeshua says,
The heavens and earth will roll up in your presence
and you who live from the living one will not see death.

Doesn't Yeshua say this?
Whoever has found oneself,
of that person the world is not worthy.

(112) Yeshua says,
Shame on the flesh that depends on the soul.
Shame on the soul that depends on the flesh.

(113) His students said to him,
When will the kingdom come?

Yeshua says,
It will not come because you are watching for it.
No one will announce, "Look, here it is,"
or "Look, there it is."
The father's kingdom is spread out upon the earth
and people do not see it.

(114) Shimon Kefa said to them,
Miryam should leave us.
Females are not worthy of life.

Yeshua says,
Look, I shall guide her to make her male,
so she too may become a living spirit resembling you males.
For every female who makes herself male
will enter the kingdom of heaven.[15]

2

THE GOSPEL OF MARY

The Gospel of Mary[1] is a wisdom gospel written in the name of Mary of Magdala, or Mary Magdalene, a beloved disciple and student of Jesus. According to the Gospel of Mary, Mary is the one closest to Jesus among the students, and she is the one who understands his mind and message. She encourages the other students when they are in despair. Jesus will be with us, Mary proclaims to them, for he has humanized us by making us truly human within. Peter and Andrew question the authority of Mary as a female teacher of revelatory wisdom, but their protests do not carry the day in the Gospel of Mary.

The Gospel of Mary is poorly preserved, and several pages of text are missing at the beginning and in the middle of the document. The original forms of the Semitic and Greek names of characters are used, and Miryam is given for Mary, Shimon Kefa for Simon Peter, and Andreas for Andrew.

∽

Students Speaking with the Savior

"Shall
matter be destroyed or not?"

The savior replied,
"Each nature and shaped thing and every creature
lives in and with each other, and will dissolve
into distinctive roots, and the nature of matter
will dissolve into the root of nature.
Whoever has ears to hear should hear."

Kefa said to him,
"You have revealed all things to us. Tell us
more. Tell us what is sin in the world?"

The savior answered,
"There is no sin, but you create sin
when you commingle as in adultery,
and this is called sin. And so the good
came to be with you, to those of every nature,
to restore each nature down to its root."

He went on:
"That's why you fall into sickness and die.
You love something and what you love tricks you.
Whoever has a mind should understand.

"Matter gave birth to passion without form
because it comes from what is against nature
and so confusion rose throughout your body.
That is why I told you, 'Be courageous.'
If you despair, stand up and gaze ahead
before nature's diversity of forms.
Whoever has ears to hear should hear."

After telling his tale, the blessed one
welcomed all of them and said,
"Peace be with you, receive my peace.

Take care that no one sends you into wrong,
saying, 'Look here, look there.'
The human child is in you. Follow
the child. If you look you will find it.
Go preach the message of good news
about the kingdom. Don't make any rules
other than what I have given you. Establish
no law as lawgivers have done, or by
those laws each one of you will be bound."

After saying these words he went away.

Miryam Consoles the Students, and Kefa Challenges Miryam

The students broke down in despair and cried deeply, saying,
"How can we go out to the gentiles and preach
the message of good news about the kingdom
of the human child? If they didn't
spare him, how possibly can we be spared?"

Miryam stood up and greeted each of them,
responding to her brothers,
"Don't cry or break down in despair or doubt.
His grace will go with you and protect you.
Rather, let us praise the greatness of his work,
for he prepared us, made us truly human."

When Miryam said this, she turned their hearts to the good,
and so they began to look into the savior's words.

Then Kefa said to Miryam,
"Sister, we know the savior loved you more

than any other woman. Tell us what
the savior told you, his words as you
remember them. Only you know them,
but we do not because we never heard them."

Miryam answered,
"What is hidden from you I shall reveal
to you."

She began to tell his words, saying,
"I saw the master[2] in a vision. I said,
'Master, today I saw you in a vision.'
He answered and told me, 'Blessings on you
since you didn't tremble when you saw me.
Where mind is the treasure is.'" I asked him,
'Master, how does one contemplate a vision?
With soul or spirit?' He answered me, saying,
'One sees neither with soul nor with the spirit.
The mind, which is between the two, sees a vision.'"

Miryam Recounts Her Vision of the Soul's Ascent

"Desire said,[3]
'I didn't see you coming down, but now
I see you rising. Tell me why you're lying,
since you belong to me.'

"The soul responded,
'I saw you but you didn't see me or know
me and for you I was nothing more than
a garment.[4] You couldn't know who I was.'

"After the soul said this, she left, intensely happy.
The soul approached the third power, called ignorance.
The power questioned the soul, saying,
'Where are you going? You are bound by evil,
you are bound, so do not judge.'

"The soul said,
'Why do you judge me? I haven't judged you.
I was roped up, but I have not bound ropes
on others. Though I wasn't recognized,
I've understood that all will be dissolved,
both what is earthly and what is heavenly.'

"When the soul overcame the third power,
she rose and saw the fourth power. It took seven forms:
The first form is darkness,
the second, desire,
the third, ignorance,
the fourth, death wish,
the fifth, a kingdom of flesh,
the sixth, foolish wisdom of flesh,
the seventh, a hothead's wisdom.

"These are the seven powers of wrath.

"The powers asked the soul, 'Where are you coming
from, you who murder mortals, and where
are you going, you who destroy realms?'

"The soul answered, saying,
'What binds me is slain and what surrounds me
 destroyed. My desire is gone. Ignorance is dead.

In a world I was freed through[5] another world.
In an image I was freed through a heavenly image.
The fetter of oblivion is temporary.
From now on I'll rest through the time of the age
in silence.'"

Kefa and Andreas Doubt Miryam's Word

When Miryam had said this, she grew silent,
for the savior had told her this much.
Andreas answered, saying to the brothers,
"Say what you will about what she said.
I still don't think the savior said this.
These teachings are very strange ideas."

Kefa expressed similar concerns.
He asked the others about the savior:
"Did he actually speak with a woman in private,
without our knowledge? Should we all now turn
and listen to her? Did he prefer her to us?"

Levi Speaks on Behalf of Miryam

Then Miryam cried and said to Kefa,
"My brother, Kefa, tell me what you think.
Do you think that I made this up myself
or that I am telling lies about the savior?"

Levi answered and said to Kefa,
"Kefa, you are always a hothead. Now I see you
arguing against this woman like an enemy.
If the savior made her worthy, who are you

to turn her away? Certainly the savior
knows her well. That is why he's loved her more
than we are loved. We should be all ashamed
and don perfect humanity and assume it
as he commanded us, and preach good news,
and never to invent a rule or law other
than what the savior has spelled out."

When Levi said this, they began to leave
to teach and preach.

3

THE GOSPEL OF JUDAS

The Gospel of Judas—that is, the Gospel of Judas Iscariot[1]—is a text that has been known by title from the comments of the heresiologist Irenaeus of Lyon but has been made available only recently. The Gospel of Judas communicates a series of conversations between Jesus and his students, and particularly Judas Iscariot. Within the text Judas is the only one of the students who understands who Jesus actually is, and he refers to Jesus, in terms familiar from gnostic and especially Sethian gnostic sources, as coming from the exalted realm of Barbelo—that is, in a name of apparent Hebrew derivation, from the realm of the highest manifestation of divinity, perhaps "god in four," god in the holy four-letter name, Yahweh. Jesus, as a revealer of wisdom, proceeds to provide for Judas a series of insights into the nature of the divine and the character of the universe, and the emergence of the cosmos is recounted in brilliant detail, from the great invisible spirit above and the angelic emanations of light to the gloomy powers of the world of mortality below, named with the Aramaic names Nebro, Yaldabaoth, and Sakla. In the end Jesus says that he has told Judas everything, and that Judas will hand over to the authorities the mortal body Jesus has been using. That is precisely what Judas does at the end of the gospel.

The Gospel of Judas has been reassembled from papyrus fragments, but lacunae or gaps remain in the manuscript. (Some lacunae have been filled with newly recovered fragments.) In this translation the Semitic name Yeshua is given for Jesus and Yehuda for Judas (or, one time, for the land of Judea), and several times *rabbi* is used for *master* (Coptic *sah*; the word *rabbi*, partially restored, is also present in one instance in the manuscript). Mihael is the angel Michael and Gavriel is the angel Gabriel. The celebration of the Pesach refers to Passover, and Adamas refers to Adam above, the ideal, heavenly human. The word *Amen* is retained in the familiar authoritative formula of Jesus, "Amen I say to you."

Secret Revelation

Here is the secret revelation Yeshua
had with Yehuda Iskariot in one week[2]
three days before the Pesach celebration.[3]

Yeshua Tells of Mysteries Beyond This World

When Yeshua came to live upon the earth
he did dynamic miracles and wonders
for the salvation of the peopled world.
While some walked in the way of justice,
others ambled about in their transgressions,
and so he called for twelve students to help.
He spoke to them about the mysteries
beyond the world and what would happen when
the end came upon them. And frequently
he wouldn't come himself before his students:
mingled among them they would find a child.[4]

Yeshua Astonishes His Students

One day in Yehuda[5] he went to his students.
He found them all sitting together as
they all were practicing group piety.
When he came near, they offered
a prayer of thanks over the bread. He laughed.

The students said, "Rabbi, why do you laugh
at us for giving thanks? Are we in error?"
He answered, saying to them, "I don't laugh
at you. You are acting not of your own will
but so that through these things your god will know
your offerings of praise." They said, "Rabbi,
you   are the son of our own god."

And Yeshua
told them, "How do you know me? Amen I say
to you, no generation of the people
who walk among you will know who I am."

Angry Students

When the students had listened to all of this,
they broke into anger and fury. They
began to execrate him in their hearts.
When Yeshua noticed their deep ignorance
and interior weakness, he asked them,
"Why has your agitation made you furious?
The god who operates inside you[6] spurs
the anger in your souls. Let any one of you
endowed with strength among human beings
produce the perfect human, and stand near

so I can gaze on him face-to-face."
They all replied to him, "We have that strength."

Here their beings of spirit didn't dare to stand
before him, except for Yehuda Iskariot.
He was able to stand before the figure
but couldn't look him in the eye and turned
his face down and away. Yehuda said,
"I know who you are and where you come from.
You are from the deathless realm of the aeon
of Barbelo, the holy source of all,
and my mouth is unworthy to utter
the ineffable name of him who sent you."

Yeshua Speaks to Yehuda Privately of His Fate

When Yeshua saw Yehuda brooding on the rest
of what is exalted, he motioned to him,
"Come here and I shall tell you mysteries
of the kingdom, not that you'll go there,
but you'll go through deep grief,
for someone will replace you to complete
the circle of the twelve before their god."
Yehuda said to him, "When will you give
me these secrets? And when will the great day
of light spread dawn upon the generation?"
But by the time he spoke, Yeshua was gone.

Yeshua Tells His Students of Earthly and Eternal Generations

Early in the morning Yeshua came again
before his students, and they said to him,
"Rabbi, after you left us you disappeared.
Where did you travel to, what did you do?"

Yeshua told them, "I went to a holy and great
dominion of another generation."
His students asked, "What is the great generation
that lies above us, holier than we are,
and one that doesn't glitter in our world?"

When Yeshua heard this, he laughed and said,
"Why are you mumbling in your hearts
about the strong and holy generation?
Amen I tell you, no one born in this aeon
will be able to glimpse that generation,
and no army of angels from the stars
will have dominion over that generation,
and no person of mortal birth can join it,
because that generation is not from
        what has come to be
the generation of the people among them,
but it is from the generation of the great people
the powerful authorities
nor any of the powers
those by which you rule."

When his students heard this, each of them sank,
spirit in turmoil, and couldn't say a word.

And on another day Yeshua came up
to be among them. And they said to him,
"Rabbi, we've seen you in a night vision,
in great dreams last night." He answered,
"Why have you fled into hiding?"[7]

The Students Envision the Temple

They said, "We've seen a giant house. It has
a great altar inside. They are the twelve men.
We think that they are priests. There is a name,
and crowds of people are waiting at the altar
till the priests present the offerings.
We were there too." Yeshua said,
"And what are these priests like?"

They answered, "Some fast for two weeks.
Some sacrifice their children, others wives,
all under ruses of humility
or praise. Some sleep with men, and others murder.
And some perform a multitude of sins
and lawless acts. And yet these men before
the altar constantly invoke your name,
and in their own deeds of sacrifice
they fill the altar with offerings."
After their speech they were silent and troubled.

Yeshua Speaks about the Temple and Sacrifices at the Altar

Yeshua said to them, "Why are you troubled?
Amen I say to you, all the priests standing
before the altar proclaim my name. Again

I say to you, my name has been set down
in writing   in the generations of the stars
through the human generations.
They operate, planting trees that bear no fruit,
shamefully, and do so in my name." He went on,
"Those whom you've seen presenting offerings
before the altar, they are the ones you are.
That is the god you serve, and you are those
twelve men you also saw. Cattle you saw
brought in for sacrifice mirror the many
people you lead astray before that same
altar. The ruler of the world[8] will stand,
using my name in such a way, and generations
of those with faith and piety stand loyal
by him. Yet after him another man
will stand before you from the fornicators,
another from the child-slayers,
another from those who sleep with men,
from those who keep the fast, and from all
the others, from among the people of pollution,
lawlessness, and error. Some say, 'We are like
angels.' They are stars bringing an end to all.
And to this generation's human beings
it is announced, 'Look, now god has received
your sacrifice from a priest's hands,' meaning
a minister of error. But it is the lord
of the universe who commands and speaks.
On the last day they will be shamed and punished."

Stop Sacrificing

Yeshua said to them, "Stop sacrificing animals.[9]
On the altar you lifted them up,

and they are over your stars with your angels,
where they already have come to their end.
So let them be of no account before you,
and let them be clear to you."

His students said, "Rabbi,
cleanse us from the
that we have done
through the deceit of the angels."

Yeshua said to them,
"It is impossible

nor can a fountain quench the fire
of the whole peopled world,
nor can a city's spring satisfy
all the generations,
except the great one, as is its destiny.
And a single lamp will not illumine
all the aeons,
except the second generation,[10]
nor can a baker feed all of creation
under heaven." When the students heard this,
they said to him, "Master, help us, save us."

The Stars

Yeshua told them, "Stop struggling with me.
Each of you has a star assigned to you
the stars will
what is his[11]
I was not sent to the corruptible generation
but to the generation

that is strong and incorruptible.
For no enemy has ruled over
that generation, nor any of the stars.
Amen I say to you, the pillar of fire
will fall quickly, and that generation
will not move   stars."
                              When Yeshua
said these things, he left
and took Yehuda Iskariot with him.
He said to him, "The water
     of the lofty mountain
     is from
     that has not come
     a spring of water for the tree
     of this aeon   after a time
     but this has come to water
god's paradise and the enduring generation,
because it won't defile the walk through life
of that generation, forever and forever."[12]

Yehuda Asks Yeshua about Bearing Fruit

Yehuda asked him, "Rabbi, what kind of fruit
does this generation yield?"
                              Yeshua replied,
"The souls of each human generation
will die. However, when these people end
the time within the kingdom
and the spirit leaves them,
their bodies die, but their souls
will stay alive, and they will be
risen above."

Yehuda asked,
"And what will all the other human generations
do?"

Yeshua said, "It is impossible
to sow seed upon rock and harvest fruit.
That is the action   of the defiled peoples
    and of wisdom that is corrupted
    the hand creating mortal people,
so their souls rise up to eternal
realms above. Amen I say to you,
no authority or angel or power can see
the realms that this great holy generation
can see."[13]

And after Yeshua spoke these words he left.

Yehuda's Vision

Yehuda said, "Rabbi, as you have heard
all the others, hear me. I've had a vision."

When Yeshua heard this, he broke into laughter
and said to him, "You who are the thirteenth
daimon,[14] why do you try so hard? But speak
to me, and I shall be here to hear you."

Yehuda told him, "In the vision I saw
myself and the twelve students stoning me
and persecuting me most grievously.
I also came to the place where   you were.
I saw a house   of such
cosmic dimension that my eyes

could not perceive the scope. Great people
surrounded it, and that house had a single
room,[15] and in the middle of the house
was a crowd
 I was saying, 'Rabbi, take me in along
with all these people.'"

Yeshua answered, saying,
"Yehuda, your star led you astray. Further,
no person of mortal birth is worthy
to go into the house that you have seen.
It's for the holy, solely for them. Neither sun
nor moon will have dominion there, nor day,
and yet the holy will live there forever
in the eternal realm with holy angels.
Look, I have revealed to you the mysteries
of the kingdom and I have taught you
about the error of the stars, and   send
on the twelve aeons."

Yehuda Asks What Will Happen to Him

Yehuda asked him, "Rabbi, could my seed,
my heritage, fall under the control of
the archons, who are rulers of this world?"

Yeshua answered, telling him, "Come here
that I may

But you know deepest sorrow when you see
the kingdom and all of its generation."

When he heard this, Yehuda said to him,
"What good to me is what I have received?

For you have set me apart
from that generation."
                                    Yeshua answered him,
saying, "You will become the thirteenth,
and you will be cursed by other generations.
In the end you will rule over them.
In the last days they will oppose you,
so you'll not rise up to the holy generation."[16]

Cosmology of the Spirit

Yeshua said, "Come here so I can teach you
        what no person has ever seen,
for there exists a great and boundless realm
whose horizons not even a generation
of angels has looked upon. And therein
is the great invisible spirit,
which no eye of an angel has ever seen,
no thought of the heart has ever comprehended,
and it was never called by any name.[17]

"Then a luminous cloud of light appeared.
The spirit said, 'Let an angel come into
being and he will become my attendant.'
A great angel, the enlightened divine
self-generated, emerged from the cloud.
Because of him four other angels came
into existence from another cloud,
and they became attendants for the angel,
the self-generated angel, who said,
'Let Adamas come into being,' and Adamas
emerged into being. And he created

the first luminary for him to reign over.
He said, 'Let angels come into being
to serve him,' and myriads suddenly came
into being. He said, 'Let an enlightened
aeon come into being,' and he came into
being. Then he created the second luminary
to reign over him, together with myriads
beyond number to serve and offer worship.
This is how he created other enlightened
aeons. He made them to reign over them,
and he created for them myriads of angels
beyond number to serve and offer worship.

Adamas and Luminaries

"Adamas was in the first luminous cloud
that no angel has ever seen among all
those who are called 'god.' He was
        after the image
        and after the likeness of the angel.
He made the incorruptible generation
of Seth appear to the twelve luminaries,
twenty-four of them.
He made seventy-two luminaries appear
in the incorruptible generation
in accordance with the spirit's will.
Then the seventy-two luminaries
made three hundred sixty luminaries
appear in the incorruptible generation,
in accordance with the spirit's will
that their number might be five for each.

"The twelve aeons of the twelve luminaries
constitute their father, with six heavens

for each aeon, so there are seventy-two
heavens for the seventy-two luminaries,
and for each of them five firmaments.
This comes to three hundred sixty
firmaments. They were given dominion
and a great army of angels beyond number,
for glory and adoration, and also
virgin spirits for glory and adoration
of all aeons, heavens, and their firmaments.

Cosmos, Chaos, and Underworld

"The entire multitude of those immortals
is called the cosmos—corruption, inviting
decay—by the father and the seventy-two
luminaries who are with the self-generated
and his seventy-two aeons. In the cosmos
appeared the first human
with his incorruptible powers. And the
aeon who appeared with his generation,
the aeon in whom are the cloud of knowledge
and the angel, is called El[18]   an aeon
and later   it was said, 'Let twelve
angels come into being to govern chaos and
the underworld.' And look, from the cloud came
an angel. His face flashed with fire, his countenance
was defiled with blood, and his name was Nebro,
meaning 'rebel'; others call him Yaldabaoth.
Another angel, Sakla, also came from the cloud.[19]
So Nebro made six angels, with Sakla,
to be his assistants, and each of these
produced twelve angels in the heavens,
each one possessing a section of the sky.[20]

Rulers and Angels of the Underworld

"The twelve rulers spoke with the twelve angels,
'Let each of you   and let them   a generation
and here are the five angels:
  The first is Seth, who is called the Christ.
  The second is Harmathoth, who is   [21]
  The third is Galila.
  The fourth is Yobel.
  The fifth is Adonaios.[22]
These are the five ruling the underworld,
and first of all they are over chaos.'[23]

Creation of People on the Earth

"Then Sakla said to his angels, 'Let us make
a human being after the likeness and after
the image.' They fashioned Adam and his wife
Eve, who in the cloud is known as Zoe,
which means 'life.' And by this name all generations
seek the man, and each of them calls the woman
by their own names. Now, Sakla didn't command
 produced, except
among the generations
which this
  The angel said to Adam,
'You shall live for a time with your children.'"

Yehuda Asks about Adam's Destiny

Yehuda said to Yeshua, "What is the value
of human life?"
Yeshua said,
"Why do you ponder these things? Adam
and his generation have lived their span
of life where he received his kingdom, and
with the longevity in keeping with his ruler."

Yehuda said to Yeshua, "Does the human spirit
die?"
Yeshua said, "This is why god told Mihael
to give the people spirits only on loan
so that they might offer service, but the great one
ordered Gavriel to grant spirits to the great
generation, with no ruler commanding it,
but their spirit and their soul. Therefore,
the other souls   "

Yeshua Speaks of the Destruction of the Wicked

"   light   chaos
seek after the spirit within you,
which you made to live
in flesh among the generations of
the angels. But god had knowledge brought
to Adam and those with him so that the kings
of chaos and the underworld might not
impose dominion over them."
Yehuda
said to Yeshua, "So what will those generations
do?"

Yeshua Explains Salvation History

Yeshua said, "Amen I say to you,
for all of them the stars bring events
to their consummation. When Sakla completes
the span of life assigned him, their first star
will sparkle with generations, and they
will finish what it is said they'd do.
They will fornicate in my name, will slay
their children, and they will
evil, and   [24]

the aeons that bring their generations
which represent them to Sakla.
After that   -rael[25] will come
bringing the twelve tribes of Israel
from   and the generations
will all serve Sakla,
also sinning in my name.
And your star will rule over
the thirteenth aeon."
                    At this Yeshua laughed.

Yehuda said, "Rabbi, why are you laughing
at us?"[26]
    Yeshua answered, saying, "I don't laugh
at you but at the error of the stars,
because these six stars are wandering about
with these five combatants,[27] and they
will all be destroyed along with their creatures."

Yehuda said to Yeshua, "Those
who have been bathed in your name,
what will they do?"

Yeshua said, "Amen I say
to you, this bathing   in my name

will destroy the entire generation[28]
of the earthly man Adam. Tomorrow
they will torment the one who bears me.[29]
Amen I say to you, no hand
of mortal human will sin against me.
Amen I say to you, Yehuda,
those who offer sacrifices to Sakla
will all   [30] since   upon the
all of them   everything evil.

Yehuda Will Surpass Them All

"But you will surpass all of them, for you
will sacrifice the man who bears me.[31]

"Already your horn is raised,
your anger is on fire,
your star has passed by,
and your heart has grown strong.[32]

"Amen I say to you, your last   become
the   of the aeon have[33]
and the kings have grown weak,
and the generations of the angels have grieved,
and those who are evil   the ruler,
since he is destroyed. And then the image
of the great generation of Adam
will be exalted. Before there was heaven,
earth, and angels, that generation coming
from the eternal realms existed. And look,

you have been told everything that is.
Raise your eyes and look at the cloud
and at the light within it and the stars
surrounding it. The star that leads the way
is your star."
　　　　　　　Yehuda raised his eyes and
saw the luminous cloud. And he entered
into it.[34] Those standing on the ground heard
a voice coming from the cloud, saying,
"　　great generation
　　image　　"

Yehuda Hands Yeshua Over

And Yehuda saw Yeshua no more.[35]
All at once there was a disturbance
among the Jews
Their high priests murmured because he[36]
had gone into the guest room to pray. Yet
some of the scribes were there, watching sharply
and carefully in order to arrest him
while at prayer. They were afraid of the Jews,
who esteemed him as a prophet. They came
near Yehuda and said to him, "What are
you doing here? You are Yeshua's student."

He answered them just as they wished.
Yehuda received some money
and then he handed Yeshua over to them. [37]

4

THE SECRET BOOK
OF JOHN

The Secret Book of John—also sometimes referred to as the Apocryphon of John[1]—is a classic work of Sethian gnostic mythology. This text presents an account of the creation, fall, and salvation of the world and the people within the world, and the account features the figure of Sophia, personified wisdom, in the role of the wisdom of god, who comes from above and whose divine light is trapped within people of gnosis in the world. The Secret Book of John explains the contrast between an all-transcendent One and an absurd and fallen world by means of an intricate mythological account of a god who emanates, creates, falls, and finally is saved.

The portions of the Secret Book of John that are presented here are taken from the opening of the text, with its revelation of the ineffable One; the middle part of the text, with its radical gnostic interpretation, in Platonic terms, of the Genesis story; and the close of the text, with the hymn of the savior. In these selections Yohanan is the form of the name used for John, Yaakov for James, Zavdai for Zebedee, and Moshe for Moses. The name of the Pharisee, Arimanios, recalls the evil Zoroastrian deity Ahriman. As in the Gospel of Judas, Barbelo is the name of the holy source of all. A number of distinctive names are given for the rulers and powers of this world, including Yaldabaoth, Sakla, and Samael for the first ruler of the world below.

The teaching of the savior, and the revelation of the mysteries and the things hidden in silence, things he taught his student Yohanan.

The Revealer Appears to Yohanan

One day when Yohanan, the brother of Yaakov, the sons of Zavdai, went up to the temple, it happened that a Pharisee named Arimanios came up to him and said to him, Where is your teacher, whom you followed?

I said to him, He has returned to the place from which he came.

The Pharisee said to me, This Nazarene has deceived you badly, filled your ears with lies, closed your minds, and turned you from the traditions of your parents.

When I, Yohanan, heard this, I turned away from the temple and went to a mountainous and barren place. I was distressed within, and I said,

How was the savior selected?

Why was he sent into the world by his father?

Who is his father who sent him?

To what kind of eternal realm shall we go?

And what was he saying when he told us,

This eternal realm to which you will go is modeled

after the incorruptible realm,

but he did not teach us what kind of realm that one is?

At the moment I was thinking about this, look, the heavens opened, all creation under heaven lit up, and the world shook. I was afraid, and look, I saw within the light someone[2] standing by me. As I was staring, it seemed to be an elderly person. Again it changed its appearance to be a youth. Not that there were several figures before me. Rather, there was a figure with several forms within the light. These forms appeared through each other, and the figure had three forms.

The figure said to me, Yohanan, Yohanan, why are you doubting? Why are you afraid? Are you not familiar with this figure? Then do not be fainthearted. I am with you always. I am the father, I am the mother, I am the child. I am the incorruptible and the undefiled one. Now I have come to teach you what is, what was, and what is to come, that you may understand what is invisible and what is visible; and to teach you about the unshakable race of perfect humankind. So now, lift up your head that you may understand the things I shall tell you today, and that you may relate them to your spiritual friends, who are from the unshakable race of perfect humankind.

The One

I asked if I might understand this, and it said to me, The One is a sovereign that has nothing over it. It is god and father of all, the invisible one that is over all, that is incorruptible, that is pure light at which no eye can gaze.

The One is the invisible spirit. We should not think of it as a god or like a god. For it is greater than a god, because it has nothing over it and no lord above it. It does not exist within anything inferior to it, since everything exists within it alone. It is eternal, since it does not need anything. For it is absolutely complete. It has never lacked anything in order to be completed by it. Rather, it is always absolutely complete in light. The One is

> illimitable, since there is nothing before it to limit it,
> unfathomable, since there is nothing before it to fathom it,
> immeasurable, since there was nothing before it to measure it,
> invisible, since nothing has seen it,
> eternal, since it exists eternally,

unutterable, since nothing could comprehend it to utter it,
unnamable, since there is nothing before it to give it a name.

The One is the immeasurable light.
Such a one beholds itself in its light.

Barbelo Appears

Now, this is the father, the One who beholds himself in the light surrounding him, which is the spring of living water, and provides all the realms. He reflects on his image everywhere, sees it in the spring of the spirit, and becomes enamored of his luminous water, for his image is in the spring of pure luminous water surrounding him.

The father's thought became a reality, and she who appeared in the presence of the father in shining light came forth. She is the first power who preceded everything and came forth from the father's mind as the forethought of all. Her light shines like the father's light; she, the perfect power, is the image of the perfect and invisible virgin spirit.[3]

She, the first power, the glory of Barbelo, the perfect glory among the realms, the glory of revelation, she glorified and praised the virgin spirit, for because of the spirit she had come forth.

She is the first thought, the image of the spirit. She became the universal womb, for she precedes everything,
the mother-father,
the first human,
the holy spirit,
the triple male,
the triple power,
the androgynous one with three names,
the eternal realm among the invisible beings,
the first to come forth.
Barbelo asked the invisible virgin spirit to give her foreknowledge,

and the spirit consented. When the spirit consented, foreknowledge appeared and stood by forethought. This is the one who came from the thought of the invisible virgin spirit.

Barbelo Conceives

The father gazed into Barbelo, with the pure light surrounding the invisible spirit, and its radiance. Barbelo conceived from it, and it produced a spark of light similar to the blessed light but not as great. This was the only child of the mother-father that had come forth, its only offspring, the only child of the father, the pure light. The invisible virgin spirit rejoiced over the light that was produced, that came forth first from the first power of the spirit's forethought, who is Barbelo. The child stood in the presence of the spirit as the spirit anointed the child. When the child received this from the spirit, at once it glorified the holy spirit and perfect forethought. Because of her it had come forth.

The child asked to be given mind as a companion to work with, and the spirit consented. When the invisible spirit consented, mind appeared and stood by the anointed, and glorified the spirit and Barbelo.

All these beings came into existence in silence.

The Fall of Sophia

Now, Sophia, who is the wisdom of insight[4] and who constitutes an eternal realm, conceived of a thought from herself, with the conception of the invisible spirit and foreknowledge. She wanted to bring forth something like herself, without the consent of the spirit, who had not given approval, without her partner and without his consideration.[5] The male did not give approval. She did not find her partner, and she considered this without the spirit's consent and without the knowledge of her partner. Nonetheless, she gave birth.

And because of the invincible power within her, her thought was not an idle thought. Something came out of her that was imperfect and different in appearance from her, for she had produced it without her partner. It did not resemble its mother and was misshapen.

When Sophia saw what her desire had produced, it changed into the figure of a snake with the face of a lion. Its eyes were like flashing bolts of lightning. She cast it away from her, outside that realm so that none of the immortals would see it. She had produced it ignorantly.

She surrounded it with a bright cloud and put a throne in the middle of the cloud so that no one would see it except the holy spirit, who is called the mother of the living. She named her offspring Yaldabaoth.

Yaldabaoth's World Order

Yaldabaoth is the first ruler, who took great power from his mother. Then he left her and moved away from the place where he was born. He took control and created for himself other realms with luminous fire, which still exists.

Yaldabaoth stationed seven kings, one for each sphere of heaven, to reign over the seven heavens, and five to reign over the depth of the abyss. He shared his fire with them, but he did not give away any of the power of the light that he had taken from his mother. For he is ignorant darkness.

When light mixed with darkness, it made the darkness shine. When darkness mixed with light, it dimmed the light and became neither light nor darkness, but rather gloom.

This gloomy ruler has three names: the first name is Yaldabaoth, the second is Sakla, the third is Samael.

He is wicked in his mindlessness that is in him. He said, I am god and there is no other god but me, since he did not know where his own strength had come from.

The rulers created seven powers for themselves, and the powers created six angels apiece, until there were 365 angels. These are the names and the corresponding appearances:

The first is Athoth and has the face of a sheep.

The second is Eloaios and has the face of a donkey.

The third is Astaphaios and has the face of a hyena.

The fourth is Yao and has the face of a snake with seven heads.

The fifth is Sabaoth and has the face of a snake.

The sixth is Adonin and has the face of an ape.

The seventh is Sabbataios and has a face of flaming fire.

This is the sevenfold nature of the week.

When he saw creation surrounding him, and the throng of angels around him who had come forth from him, he said to them, I am a jealous god and there is no other god beside me.

But by announcing this, he suggested to the angels with him that there is another god. For if there were no other god, of whom would he be jealous?

Sophia Repents

Then the mother began to move around. She realized that she was lacking something when the brightness of her light diminished. She grew dim because her partner had not collaborated with her.

The arrogant one took power from his mother. He was ignorant, for he thought no one existed except his mother alone. When he saw the throng of angels he had created, he exalted himself over them.

When the mother realized that the trappings[6] of darkness had come into being imperfectly, she understood that her partner had not collaborated with her. She repented with many tears. The whole realm of fullness heard her prayer of repentance and offered praise on her behalf to the invisible virgin spirit, and the spirit consented. When the invisible spirit consented, the holy spirit poured upon her some of the fullness of all. For her partner did not come to her on his own, but he came to her through the realm of fullness, so that he might restore what she lacked. She was taken up not to her own eternal realm, but to a position above her son. She was to remain in the ninth heaven until she restored what was lacking in herself.

The Human Appears

A voice called from the exalted heavenly realm,
> The human exists
> and the human child.

The first ruler, Yaldabaoth, heard the voice and thought it had come from his mother. He did not realize its source. The holy perfect mother-father, the first human—this is the one who showed them, and appeared in human shape.

The entire realm of the first ruler quaked, and the foundations of the abyss shook. The bottom of the waters above the material world was lighted by this image that had appeared. When the authorities and the first ruler stared at this appearance, they saw the shape of the image in the water.

The Creation of Adam

Yaldabaoth said to the authorities with him, Come, let us create a human being after the image of god and with a likeness to ourselves, so that this human image may give us light.

They created through their respective powers, according to the features that were given to them. Each of the authorities contributed a psychical feature corresponding to the figure of the image they had seen. They created a being like the perfect first human and said, Let us call it Adam, that its name may give us power of light.

Adam Receives Spirit and Life

All the angels and demons worked together until they fashioned the psychical body. But for a long time their creation did not stir or move at all.

When the mother wanted to take back the power she had relinquished to the first ruler, she prayed to the most merciful mother-father of all. With a sacred command the mother-father sent five luminaries down to the place of the angels of the first ruler. They advised him so that they might recover the mother's power.

They said to Yaldabaoth, Breathe some of your spirit into the face of Adam, and then the body will arise.

He breathed his spirit into Adam. The spirit is the power of his mother, but he did not realize this, because he lives in ignorance. The mother's power went out of Yaldabaoth and into the psychical body that had been made to be like the one who is from the beginning. The body moved and became powerful. And it was enlightened.

At once the rest of the powers became jealous. Although Adam had come into being through all of them, and they had given their power to this human, Adam was more intelligent than the creators and the first ruler. When they realized that Adam was enlightened, and could think more clearly than they, and was stripped of evil, they took and threw Adam into the lowest part of the whole material realm.

The blessed, benevolent, merciful mother-father had compassion for the mother's power that had been removed from the first ruler. The rulers might be able to overpower the psychical, perceptible body once again. So with its benevolent spirit and great mercy the mother-father sent a helper to Adam, an enlightened insight who is from the mother-father and who was called life. She helped the whole creature, laboring with it, restoring it to its fullness, teaching it about the descent of the seed, teaching it about the way of ascent, which is the way of descent.

Enlightened insight was hidden within Adam so that the rulers might not recognize her, but that insight might be able to restore what the mother lacked.

The Imprisonment of Humanity

The human being Adam was revealed through the bright shadow within. And Adam's ability to think was greater than that of all the creators. When they looked up, they saw that Adam's ability to think was greater, and they devised a plan with the whole throng of rulers and angels. They took fire, earth, and water, and combined them with the four fiery winds. They wrought them together and made a great commotion.[7]

The rulers brought Adam into the shadow of death so that they might produce a figure again, from earth, water, fire, and the spirit that comes from matter, that is, from the ignorance of darkness, and desire, and their own false spirit. This is the cave for remodeling the body that these criminals put on the human, the fetter of forgetfulness.[8] Adam became a mortal being, the first to descend and the first to become estranged.

The enlightened insight within Adam, however, would rejuvenate Adam's mind.

The rulers took Adam and put Adam in paradise. They said, Eat, meaning, do so in a leisurely manner. But in fact their pleasure is bitter and their beauty is perverse. Their pleasure is a trap, their trees are a sacrilege, their fruit is deadly poison, their promise is death.

They put their tree of life in the middle of paradise.

I[9] shall teach you the secret of their life, the plan they devised together, the nature of their spirit: The root of their tree is bitter, its branches are death, its shadow is hatred, a trap is in its leaves, its blossom is bad ointment, its fruit is death, desire is its seed, it blossoms in darkness. The dwelling place of those who taste of it is the underworld, and darkness is their resting place.

But the rulers lingered in front of what they call the tree of the knowledge of good and evil, which is the enlightened insight,[10] so that Adam might not behold its fullness and recognize his shameful nakedness.

But I[11] was the one who induced them to eat.

I[12] said to the savior, Master, was it not the snake that instructed Adam to eat?

The savior laughed and said, The snake instructed them to eat of the wickedness of sexual desire and destruction so that Adam might be of use to the snake. This is the one who knew Adam was disobedient because of the enlightened insight within Adam, which made Adam stronger of mind than the first ruler. The first ruler wanted to recover the power that he himself had passed on to Adam. So he brought deep sleep upon Adam.

I said to the savior, What is this deep sleep?

The savior said, It is not as Moshe wrote and you heard. He said in his first book, He put Adam to sleep. Rather, this deep sleep was a loss of sense. Thus the first ruler said through the prophet, I shall make their minds sluggish, that they may neither understand nor discern.

The Creation of Eve

Enlightened insight hid herself within Adam. The first ruler wanted to take her from Adam's side, but enlightened insight cannot be apprehended. While darkness pursued her, it did not apprehend her. The first ruler removed part of Adam's power and created another figure in the form of a female, like the image of insight that had appeared to him. He put the part he had taken from the power of the human being into the female creature. It did not happen, however, the way Moshe said: Adam's rib.

Adam saw the woman beside him. At once enlightened insight appeared and removed the veil that covered his mind. He sobered up from the drunkenness of darkness. He recognized his counterpart and said, This is now bone from my bones and flesh from my flesh.

For this reason a man will leave his father and his mother and will join himself to his wife, and the two of them will become one flesh. For his partner will be sent to him, and he will leave his father and his mother.

Our sister Sophia is the one who descended in an innocent manner to restore what she lacked. For this reason she was called life, that is, the mother of the living, by the forethought of the sovereignty of heaven and by the insight that appeared to Adam. Through her have the living tasted perfect knowledge.

As for me, I appeared in the form of an eagle[13] on the tree of knowledge, which is the insight of the pure enlightened forethought, that I might teach the human beings and awaken them from the depth of sleep. For the two of them were fallen and realized that they were naked. Insight appeared to them as light and awakened their minds.

Yaldabaoth Defiles Eve

When Yaldabaoth realized that the humans had withdrawn from him, he cursed his earth. He found the woman as she was preparing herself for her husband. He was master over her. And he did not know the mystery that had come into being through the sacred plan. The two of them were afraid to denounce Yaldabaoth. He displayed to his angels the ignorance within him. He threw the humans out of paradise and cloaked them in thick darkness.

The first ruler saw the young woman standing next to Adam and noticed that the enlightened insight of life had appeared in her. Yet Yaldabaoth was full of ignorance. So when the forethought of all realized this, she dispatched emissaries, and they stole life out of Eve.

The first ruler defiled Eve and produced in her two sons, a first and a second: Elohim and Yahweh.[14]

> Elohim has the face of a bear,
> Yahweh has the face of a cat.
> One is just, the other is unjust.
> He placed Yahweh over fire and wind,
> he placed Elohim over water and earth.
> He called them by the names Cain and Abel, with a view to
> deceive.

To this day sexual intercourse has persisted because of the first ruler. He planted sexual desire in the woman who belongs to Adam. Through intercourse the first ruler produced duplicate bodies, and he blew some of his false spirit into them.

He placed these two rulers over the elements so that they might rule over the cave.

When Adam came to know the counterpart of his own foreknowledge, he produced a son like the human child. He called him Seth, after the manner of the heavenly race in the eternal realms. Similarly, the mother sent down her spirit, which is like her and is a copy of what is in the realm of fullness, for she was going to prepare a dwelling place for the eternal realms that would come down.

The human beings were made to drink water of forgetfulness[15] by the first ruler, so that they might not know where they had come from. For a time the seed remained and helped so that when the spirit descends from the holy realms, it may raise up the seed and heal what it lacks, that the entire realm of fullness may be holy and lack nothing.

Hymn of the Savior

Now I, the perfect forethought of all, transformed myself into my offspring. I existed first and went down every path.[16]

I am the abundance of light,

I am the remembrance of fullness.

I went into the realm of great darkness and continued until I entered the midst of the prison. The foundations of chaos shook, and I hid from them because of their evil, and they did not recognize me.

Again I returned, a second time, and went on. I had come from the inhabitants of light—I, the remembrance of forethought.

I entered the midst of darkness and the bowels of the underworld, turning to my task. The foundations of chaos shook as though to fall upon those who dwell in chaos and destroy them. Again I hurried back to the root of my light so they might not be destroyed before their time.

Again, a third time, I went forth—

I am the light dwelling in light,

I am the remembrance of forethought—

so that I might enter the midst of darkness and the bowels of the underworld. I brightened my face with light from the consummation of their realm and entered the midst of their prison, which is the prison of the body.

I said, Let whoever hears arise from deep sleep.

A person wept and shed tears. Bitter tears the person wiped away, and said, Who is calling my name? From where has my hope come as I dwell in the bondage of prison?

I said,

I am the forethought of pure light,

I am the thought of the virgin spirit, who raises you to a place of honor.

Arise, remember that you have heard

and trace your root,

which is I, the compassionate.

Guard yourself against the angels of misery,

the demons of chaos and all who entrap you,

and beware of deep sleep

and the trap in the bowels of the underworld.

I raised and sealed the person in luminous water with five seals, that death might not prevail over the person from that moment on.

Conclusion

Look, now I shall ascend to the perfect realm. I have finished everything for you in your hearing. I have told you everything for you to record and communicate secretly to your spiritual friends. This is the mystery of the unshakable race.

The savior communicated this to Yohanan for him to record and safeguard. He said to him, Cursed be anyone who will trade these things for a gift, for food, drink, clothes, or anything like this.

These things were communicated to Yohanan in a mystery, and at once the savior disappeared. Then Yohanan went to the other students and reported what the savior had told him.

5

ON THE ORIGIN OF THE WORLD

The text given the title On the Origin of the World[1] offers a cosmological account of the creation of the world, its fall, and the eventual salvation of the light that has found its way into the world. On the Origin of the World is a smart, scholarly essay on various themes in a gnostic worldview. The text addresses many of the same topics as the Secret Book of John, and it includes a song of Eve that closely follows lines of poetry in the next text in this collection, Thunder.

The selection from the essay On the Origin of the World given here portrays in colorful terms the creation of paradise and human beings in paradise. The narrative recalls the story as told in Genesis, but with a remarkably different interpretation. Here exalted Eve is the woman who makes Adam rise and come to life, and Sophia is the heavenly mother who orchestrates the salvation of the people of light.

Within the passage that is translated are the names Pistis, "faith" in Greek, referring to Pistis Sophia, "faith wisdom"; Sabaoth, "armies" or "hosts" in Hebrew (as in "lord of hosts"), referring to the repentant son of the demiurge Yaldabaoth; and Zoe, "life" in Greek, referring to Sophia Zoe or heavenly Eve.

Justice created beautiful paradise.² Paradise lies outside the circuit of the moon and the circuit of the sun in the luxuriant earth, which is in the east in the rocky region. Desire dwells in the midst of trees, since they are beautiful and appealing.

Now, the color of the tree of life is like the sun, and its branches are lovely. Its leaves are like those of the cypress, and its fruit is like a cluster of white grapes. Its height reaches up to heaven. Next to it is the tree of knowledge, endowed with the power of god. Its glory is like the moon shining brightly, and its branches are lovely. Its leaves are like fig leaves, and its fruit is like a bunch of good, delicious dates. This tree is planted in the north of paradise to raise up souls from demonic stupor, so they might come to the tree of life and eat its fruit and condemn the authorities and their angels.

The Creation of People

Before Adam of light made his return, the authorities caught a glimpse of him in chaos. They laughed at the chief creator, for he lied when he said, "I am god. There is none before me."

When they came to the chief creator, they said, "Isn't this being the god who ruined what we have done?"

He answered, "Yes it is. If you do not want him to be able to ruin our work, come, let's fashion a human being from earth in the image of our bodies and with a likeness to this being,³ to serve us, so that when this being sees someone like him, he may fall in love. Then he will stop ruining what we have done, and we can enslave the children born from the light for this whole age."

All these things took place according to the forethought of Pistis, so that humanity might come to look like this being and condemn the authorities because of their molded bodies. For within their molded bodies was the light.

The authorities got the knowledge needed to create humanity. Sophia Zoe, who dwells with Sabaoth, anticipated their actions. She

laughed at their plan, for they are blind, and they created people ignorantly, contrary to their own interests. They had no idea what they
were doing.

She anticipated them. She created her own person first, before
them, so that this person might instruct the molded bodies of the
authorities how they might scorn them and escape them.

The birth of this instructor was as follows. Sophia let a drop of
light fall, and it landed on the water, and at once an androgynous
human being appeared. First Sophia made the drop into the form of
a woman's body, and then she took the body and made it into a shape
resembling the mother who had appeared. It took her twelve months
to complete it.

A human androgyne was born, the one Greeks call Hermaph-
rodite. Jews call this child's mother Eve of life,[4] that is, the female
instructor of life, and her child is the lord. Later the authorities called
the child the beast, to fool their molded bodies. The beast, however,
is understood to be the instructor, for it was found to be the wisest of
creatures.[5]

The Song of Eve

Eve is the first virgin, and she gave birth to her child without any
man. She acted as her own physician. That is why it is said that she
announced,

> "I am part of my mother, I am mother.
> I am the wife, I am the virgin.
> I am pregnant, I am the physician.
> I am the comforter of labor pains.
> My husband produced me,
> I am his mother,
> and he is my father and lord.
> He is my strength;

what he wants he explains with reason.
I am becoming,
but I have borne a lordly man."[6]

These things were revealed through the will of Sabaoth and his anointed to the souls who were about to enter the molded bodies of the authorities. The holy voice said of them, "Be fruitful and multiply; rule over all creatures." These souls were seized, in keeping with their fates, by the chief creator, and they were imprisoned in molded bodies, until the end of the age.

The World Rulers Form Adam

Then the chief creator offered his opinion about humanity to those with him, and each of them cast his semen into the midst of the navel of the earth.

Since that time the seven rulers formed people with a body resembling their bodies, but the likeness of people is linked to the human being who appeared to the rulers. The molded body came to be, one part at a time, from each one of the rulers, and their leader created the brain and marrow.

After that the person came to appear like the one before him. He came to be a person of soul, and he was named Adam, meaning father, after the name of the one before him.

When Adam had been made, the chief creator abandoned him as a vessel devoid of life, since Adam was formed like an aborted fetus, without spirit. When the chief creator remembered the word of Pistis, he feared that the true human being might enter his molded body and rule over it. For this reason he left his molded body forty days without soul, and he went away and left him.

On the fortieth day, Sophia Zoe blew her breath into Adam, who had no soul. Adam began to crawl around on the ground, but he was unable to stand up.

The seven rulers came and saw him, and they were deeply disturbed. They came up to him and took hold of him, and the chief creator addressed the breath that was in him: "Who are you? Where are you from?"

He answered, "I have come through the power of the human being in order to destroy your work."

When they heard this, they praised him, because he provided them rest from their fears and worries.[7] They called that day the day of rest, because they found rest from their troubles.

They saw that Adam could not stand up, and they were happy. They took him and placed him in paradise, and they retired up to their heavens.

Eve Gives Adam Life

After the day of rest, Sophia sent her daughter Zoe, referred to as Eve, as an instructor to raise Adam, who had no soul, so that the children he would produce would be vessels of light.

When Eve saw her male companion on the ground, she pitied him and said, "Adam, come to life. Rise up from the ground."

Immediately her command came to pass. Adam rose up, and at once he opened his eyes, saw Eve, and said, "You shall be called the mother of the living, for you have given me life."

The Rape of Earthly Eve by the Chief Creator and His Angels

The authorities learned that their molded body was alive and had risen up, and they were greatly disturbed. They dispatched seven archangels to find out what happened.

They approached Adam, and when they saw Eve speaking with him, they talked among themselves. "Who is this enlightened woman?

She looks just like the being that appeared to us in the light. Come, let's grab her and cast our semen into her, so that she may be polluted and unable to go up to her light, and her children will serve us. And let's not tell Adam, since he is not one of us. Rather, let us make him fall asleep and hint in his sleep that Eve has come from his rib, so that the woman may serve and he may rule over her."

Now, Eve was a power from heaven, and so she laughed at their plans. She darkened their eyes and secretly left her likeness there with Adam.

She entered the tree of knowledge and lingered there. The rulers pursued her, and she showed them that she had entered the tree and had become the tree. The powers, blind as they were, were very fearful, and they ran away.[8]

At a later time, when they regained their sight, they came up to Adam. They saw someone who looked like that woman with him, and they were upset, supposing this to be the true Eve. They were desperate. They approached her, grabbed her, and cast their semen on her.

The powers did wicked things. They debauched her in ways that were not only natural but also obscene, first by defiling the seal of her voice, which had asked them, "What is it that exists before you?"[9] In this manner they also intended to defile those who maintain that they were born through the word, through the true human, at the end of the age.

The powers made a huge mistake. They did not know that they had defiled their own body. The authorities and their angels defiled the likeness in every conceivable way.

Eve Gives Birth to Children of the Powers

First Eve conceived Abel from the first ruler, then she bore the other children from the seven authorities and their angels.

These things occurred according to the forethought of the chief creator, in order that the first mother might bear within herself the seed of the offspring, all commingled and connected with the fate of the world and its arrangements and legal enactments.

A plan emerged for Eve, so that the molded bodies of the authorities might function to contain the light. Then the light would condemn the authorities through their own molded bodies.

The original Adam of light is spiritual, and he appeared on the first day. The second Adam is psychical, a person of soul, and he appeared on the sixth day, named Aphrodite. The third Adam is earthly, a person of dust and law, and he appeared on the eighth day, Sunday, right after the lesser day of rest.[10]

The offspring of earthly Adam multiplied and filled the earth. They gained all the technical ability of Adam with soul. But they remained in ignorance.

The Trees and the Beast

Let me go on.[11]

When the rulers noticed that Adam and the woman with him remained in error and ignorance, like animals, they were delighted.

But then they discovered that the immortal human being was not going to leave them alone, and they would also have to fear the woman who became a tree. They were dismayed and said, "Is this the one who darkened our eyes and informed us about the defiled woman who is like him, the true human, in order to defeat us?"

The seven plotted together. They approached Adam and Eve cautiously and said to him, "Feel free to eat the fruit of every tree created for you in paradise, but beware, don't eat of the tree of knowledge. If you eat, you will die." They frightened them greatly, and returned to their authorities.

The beast, wisest of creatures, stopped by. The beast saw the likeness of their mother Eve and said to her, "What is it god said to you—'Don't eat from the tree of knowledge'?"

She replied, "He not only said 'Don't eat from it' but also 'Don't touch it or you will die.'"

The beast told her, "Don't be afraid. You surely will not die. He knows that when you eat of it your minds will become sober and you will be like gods, knowing the difference between the evil and the good. He gave you this warning because he is jealous, and he wants to keep you from eating from it."

Eve believed the words of the instructor. She stared at the tree and saw that it was lovely and appealing, and she felt a desire for it. She picked some of its fruit and ate it, and she gave some to her husband as well, and he also ate. Then their minds opened.

> When they ate,
> the light of knowledge enlightened them.
> When they dressed in shame,
> they knew they were stripped of knowledge.
> When they became sober of mind,
> they recognized they were naked
> and they loved each other.
> When they saw that their makers
> looked like beasts,
> they despised them.

Adam and Eve were filled with understanding.

Finally, Light Will Overcome Darkness

Light will overcome darkness and obliterate it.[12] It will be as if the darkness never was, and the source of darkness will be gone. Deficiency will be plucked out at its root and thrown down into the darkness, and light will return to its root above.

The glory of the unconceived will become manifest and fill all the aeons when the prophets and the writings of rulers are disclosed and

fulfilled by those called perfect. Those who have not come to be perfect in the unconceived father will be glorified in their aeons and the
kingdoms of those who are immortal, but they will never enter the
realm with no king over it.

All must return to where they came from. All will reveal their
natures by what they say and know.

6

THUNDER

Thunder, or Thunder: Perfect Mind,[1] is a sacred poem of paradox and antithesis. Gnostic themes, such as liberation from the material world, a pantheistic deity that permeates matter and life, and the promise of salvation of return inform the poem, and some scholars consider these themes to echo a Sethian gnostic perspective. The speaker of the poetic lines of Thunder is female, and while there are diverse views of her identity, she may be compared with Sophia, the personified wisdom of god, revealing herself, commonly with paradoxical "I am" statements, to all who will hear.

I was dispatched from the power
    and have come to you who study me
    and am found by you who seek me.
Look at me, you who study me,
    and you who hear, pay attention to me.
You waiting for me, take me to yourselves.
Don't banish me from your sight.
Don't let hatred enter your voice against me
    nor let anger enter your hearing.

In no place, in no time, be unknowing of me.
Be alert. Don't be ignorant of me.

I am the first and last.
I am the honored and scorned.
I am the whore and holy.
I am the wife and virgin.
I am the mother and daughter.
I am the members of my mother.
I am a barren one with many sons.
I have had a splendid wedding
    and have not embraced a husband.
I am a midwife and do not give birth.
I am the solace of my birth pains.
I am bride and groom,
    and my husband engendered me.
I am the mother of my father
    and sister of my husband,
    and he is my offspring.
I am the servant of him who fashioned me.
I am the ruler of my offspring.
He produced me prematurely,
    and he is my offspring born on time,
    and from him is my strength.
I am the staff of his power in his youth
    and he the rod of my advanced years,
    and whatever he wants happens to me.
I am silence incomprehensible
    and insight with fine memory.
I am the voice whose sounds are many
    and the word whose appearances are multiple.
I am the utterance of my name.

Why do you who hate me, love me
    and hate those who love me?
You who deny me, confess me,
    and you who confess me, deny me.
You who tell the truth about me, lie about me,
    and you who lie, tell the truth.
You who know me,
        be ignorant of me,
        and those who have not known me,
        let them know me.

For I am knowledge and ignorance.
I am shy and bold.
I am shameless, I ashamed.
I am strength, I am fear.
I am war and peace.

Listen to what I say.
I am disgraced and grand.
Note my poverty and wealth.
Don't be arrogant toward me
        when I am cast down on the ground,
        and you will find me
        in those who are to come.
If you see me lying on a dung heap,
        don't run away and leave me there.
In the kingdoms you will find me.
If you see me when I am cast with the disgraced
        in the most filthy places,
        don't laugh at me.
Don't discard me with those in need.
I am compassionate, I cruel.
Be careful.

Don't hate my obedience,
>   but love my self-control.
When I am weak, don't forsake me,
>   don't fear my power.

Why do you despise my fear
>   and curse my pride?
I am a woman present in every fear
>   and I am strength in agitation.
I am a woman, weak,
>   and I am carefree in a pleasant place.
I am senseless, I am wise.
Why have you hated me in your counsels?
Because I will be silent among the silent
>   and appear and speak?
Greeks, why do you hate me?
Because I am a barbarian among the barbarians?

For I am the wisdom[2] of Greeks and knowledge of barbarians.
I am the judgment of Greeks and barbarians.
My image is great in Egypt, and I have no image among the
>   barbarians.
I am hated everywhere and loved everywhere.
I am called life[3] and you have called me death.
I am called law and you have called me lawless.
I am one you pursued, and I am one you seized.
I am one you scattered, and you gathered me together.
I am one before whom you are ashamed,
>   and to me you are shameless.
I am a woman who attends no festival,
>   and I am she whose festivals are many.
I am godless, and I have many a god.
I am one you confessed and you scorn me.
I am unlettered and you learn from me.

I am one you despise and you confess me.
I am one you hide from and you appear to me.
When you hide I show.
When you appear I hide.

As for those who have behaved foolishly,
take me from their understanding, from grief,
and accept me, from understanding and grief.
Receive me from what is lowly in creation,
    and take from the good, even though in lowliness.
Out of shame take me to yourselves shamelessly.
Without shame and with shame, put to shame
    what is mine in you.

Come to me, you who know me
    and you who know my members,
    and make great ones among small first creatures.
Come to childhood
    and don't despise it because it is small and tiny.
Don't make the great turn, piece by piece, from the small,
    for the small is known from the great.
Why do you curse and honor me?
You wound me and have mercy.
Don't separate me from the first you have known.
Don't cast out or turn away

Turn away and do not know
    what is mine.
I know the first ones,
    and those after them know me.

I am perfect mind and rest
I am the knowledge of my quest,
    the discovery of those who look for me,

the command of those who ask of me,
the power of powers, through my knowledge,
of angels, through my word,
of gods among gods, through my counsel,
of spirits of all who dwell with me,
of women who dwell within me.

I am honored, praised, and scornfully despised.
I am peace, and war has come because of me.
I am alien and citizen.
I am substance and a woman of no substance.
Those connected to me are ignorant of me,
    and those one with my being know me.
Those close to me are ignorant of me,
    and those far away have known me.
On the day I am close to you, you are far away,
    and on the day I am far away, I am close to you.

I am   the heart's lamp.
I am   of natures.
I am   of the creation of spirits,
    the request of souls.
I am control and uncontrollable.
I am union and dissolution.
I abide and dissolve.
I am descent, and people come up to me.
I am judgment and acquittal.
I am sinless,
    and the root of sin comes from me.
I am desire outwardly, yet within me is control.
I am hearing for all, and my speech cannot be grasped.
I am an unspeaking mute
    and enormous in my many words.

Hear me in gentleness
    and learn from me in roughness.

I am the woman crying out
    and I am cast upon the face of the earth.
I prepare bread and my mind within.
I am knowledge of my name.
I am the one who cries out
    and I listen.
I appear   walk in
    utterance   refutation.
I am judge, I am defense.
I am called justice, but my name is violence.

You the vanquishing honor me,
    and you the vanquished whisper against me.
Judge before you are judged,
    because in you the judge and partiality exist.
If you are condemned by one, who will acquit you?
If acquitted by one, who will arrest you?
What is in you is outside,
    and one who fashions you on the outside
    shapes you inside.
    What you see outside you see within you.
It is visible and your garment.

Hear me, listeners,
    and learn my words, you who know me.

I am the hearing all can reach;
I am speech that cannot be grasped.
I am the name of the sound
    and the sound of the name.

I am the sign of the letter
   and the designation of the division.
I   light   and shadow.
Hear me, listeners,
       take me to yourselves.
As the lord the great power lives,
   the one who stands will not change the name.
The one who stands created me.
   I will speak his name.

Look at the words of this one
   and all the writings completed.
Be alert, hearers and angels and those sent
   and you spirits arisen from the dead.
I alone exist and have no one to judge me.
Many pleasures exist in many sins,
    uncontrolled passions and disgraceful desires
    and fleeting pleasures
    embraced by people until they sober up
    and float up to their place of rest.
There they will find me and live, and they will not die again.

7

THE GOSPEL OF PHILIP

The Gospel of Philip[1] is a Valentinian anthology of Christian meditations on themes having to do with gnosis. The meditations take various forms: there are aphorisms, parables, dialogues, and sayings of
Jesus. Among the themes addressed in the brief selection given here
are light and darkness, life and death, conceiving with a kiss, embrac-
ing wisdom and Mary of Magdala, observing sacraments and the
bridal chamber, and wearing the garment of light. According to the
Gospel of Philip, Christ the anointed takes different forms for different people, yet he becomes great—and by beholding Christ, one
becomes Christ.

As in other texts, the Semitic name Yeshua is used for Jesus and
Miryam for Mary.

~

Light and Darkness

Light and darkness, life and death, on the right and left,
these are children, they are inseparably together.
But the good are not good, the wicked not wicked,
life not life, death not death.

Each element fades to an original source.
But those who live above the world cannot fade.
They are eternal.

Conceiving with a Kiss

The heavenly man has more children
than a man on earth. If the offspring of Adam
are many and die,
how many more are the offspring of the perfect man
who do not die and are born each second!
The father makes a child.
The child cannot make a son. He has not the power
to make children. One recently born is not a parent.
The son has brothers and sisters, not children.
In this world there is a natural order to birth,
and one is nourished by ordinary means.
We are nourished by the promise of heaven.
If we are from the mouth of the word,
we are nourished from the mouth, and are perfect.
By a kiss the perfect conceive and give birth.
That is why we kiss.
From the grace in others we conceive.

God Is a Dyer

God is a dyer.
The good dyes, true dyes, dissolve into things
dyed in them.
So too for things god has dyed.
His dyes are imperishable because of their colors.
What god dips he dips in water.

Seeing

It is impossible to see anything in the real realm
unless you become it.
Not so in the world. You see the sun without being the sun,
see sky and earth but are not them.
This is the truth of the world.
In the other truth you are what you see.
If you see spirit, you are spirit.
If you look at Christ the anointed, you are Christ the
    anointed.
If you see the father, you will be father.
In this world you see everything but yourself,
but there, you look at yourself and are what you see.

Pearl in the Mud

If a pearl is thrown into mud, it loses no value,
and if rubbed with balsam oil, it gains no value.
It always is precious in its owner's eyes.
Wherever they are, the children of god
are precious in the eyes of the father.

Wisdom and Miryam of Magdala

Wisdom,[2] who is called "barren," is mother of the angels.
The companion of the savior is Miryam of Magdala.
The savior loved her more than all his students
and kissed her often on her mouth.[3]
The others said, "Why do you love her more than us?"
The savior answered, saying to them,

"Why do I not love you like her? If a blind man
and one who sees are together in darkness,
they are the same.
When light comes, the one who sees will see light.
The blind man stays in darkness."

Being

The lord said, "Blessings on you
who were before you came into being.
Whoever is, was, and will be."

Marriage

Great is the mystery of marriage! Without it,
the world would not be.
The existence of the world depends
on marriage.
Think of pure sex. It possesses deep powers,
though its image is defiled.

Five Sacraments

The lord did everything through mystery:
baptism and chrism and eucharist
and redemption and bridal chamber.

Things Below Like Things Above

The lord said, "I came to make things below
like things above, and the outside like the inside.
I came to join them in one place."
He spoke here through symbols and images.
Those who say, "There is a heavenly person
and one even higher," are wrong.
Who is seen in heaven is the heavenly person,
whom they call "lower,"
and the one to whom the hidden belongs
they call "higher."
It is best to say "inner" and "outer" and "what is beyond the
    outer."
So the lord called destruction "the outer darkness."
There is nothing beyond.
He said, "My father who is in secret."
He said, "Go into the chamber and shut the door behind you,
and pray to your father who is in secret,"
the one who is innermost.
What is innermost is the fullness.[4]
Beyond it there is nothing inside.
This is the place they call "the uppermost."

Places of the Spirit

Before Christ the anointed, some came from a realm
they could not reenter,
and they went where they could not come out.
Then Christ came.
Those who went in he took out.
Those who went out he took in.

Eve in Adam

When Eve was in Adam there was no death.
When she was cut from him,
death came into being.
If she enters him again and he takes her in,
death will disappear.

Garment of Light

The perfect human can neither be grasped nor seen.
If they see him, they can grasp him,
so there is no way to grace but to put on
the perfect light and become perfect.
All who put on that garment will enter the place of rest.
This is the perfect light.
We must become perfect before leaving this world.
Who is rich and has not thrown it off
will not share in the kingdom
but will go as imperfect into the middle.
Only Yeshua knows where that will end.

The Perfect Light

As long as the seed of the holy spirit is hidden, wickedness is
    ineffectual,
but it has not yet been removed from the midst of the seed
of the holy spirit.
Everyone is a slave of evil.
But when the seed is revealed, the perfect light will flow out
    on everyone.

And all those who are in the light will receive the chrism.
Then the slaves will be free and the captives ransomed.
"Every plant that my heavenly father has not planted will be
    uprooted."
Those who are separated will be joined,
and those who are empty will be filled.

Eternal Light

Everyone who enters the bridal chamber will kindle the light,
for it burns just as in marriages performed,
    though they happen at night.
That fire burns only at night and is put out.
Yet the mysteries of this marriage are perfected
rather in the day and the light.
Neither that day nor its light ever sets.
If you become an attendant of the bridal chamber,
you will receive the light.
If you do not receive it while in this place,
you cannot receive it in the other place.
You who receive the light will not be seen nor grasped.
And no one will be able to torment you
even while you live in the world.
And when you leave the world
you have already received the truth in the images.
The world has become the eternal realm,
because the eternal realm is fullness for you.
This is the way it is. It is revealed to you alone,
not hidden in the darkness and the night
but in a perfect day and a holy light.

8

THE GOSPEL OF TRUTH

The Gospel of Truth[1] is a gnostic sermon on the saving knowledge of god. The title of this text is referred to in the writings of Irenaeus of Lyon, and it is also mentioned in the opening of the document itself. The Gospel of Truth is thought by a number of scholars to have been composed by the gnostic teacher Valentinos. Valentinos was one of the great creative minds of the second century, and from him the Valentinian school of gnostic thought eventually developed. The Gospel of Truth proclaims a mystical vision of Jesus, and the text makes use of metaphor, parable, interpretation, and elaboration to announce the way to god and knowledge of god. In the Gospel of Truth the fruit of knowledge brings joy, and signifies that one finds god in oneself. When the fog of error and terror is gone, the nightmare of darkness is replaced with an eternal heavenly day.

Key portions of the Gospel of Truth are translated here. As in other early texts in this collection, the Semitic name Yeshua is given for Jesus.

Joy for Those Who Know the Father

The gospel of truth is joy for those to whom the father of truth has given the grace of knowing him through the power of the word. The word has come from the fullness and is in the father's thought and mind. The word is called "savior," a name that refers to the work he must do for the redemption of those who have not known the father. The name "gospel" refers to the revelation of hope, because it is the means of discovery for those who seek him.

Ignorance of the Father Brings Error

All[2] sought him from whom they came. All were inside him, that illimitable, inconceivable one, who is better than every thought. But ignorance of the father brought terror and fear. Terror turned dense like a fog. No one could see. So error grew strong. She worked on her material substance and failed. She did not know truth. She assumed a fashioned figure while she prepared, in power and beauty, a substitute for truth.

It was no humiliation for the illimitable, inconceivable one. They were nothing, this terror and forgetting and this figure of falsehood, whereas established truth is unchanging, unperturbed, and completely beautiful.

So don't take error seriously.

Error had no root and was in a fog about the father. She prepared works and accomplished acts of forgetting and fears to beguile those of the middle and capture them. Error's forgetting was not revealed. It is not from the father.[3] Forgetting did not come into being from the father, though if it did come into being, it is because of the father.[4] In him is knowledge, revealed so forgetting might be destroyed and the father known. Forgetting came because the father was not known. When the father is known, forgetting will be gone.

Yeshua Is the Fruit of Knowledge

That is the gospel of him they seek, which is revealed to the perfect through the father's mercies. Through the hidden mystery Yeshua the anointed enlightened those who were in darkness because of forgetting. He enlightened them and gave them a path. And that path is the truth he taught them.

Error was angry with him and persecuted him. He distressed her and she was powerless. He was nailed to a tree. He became a fruit of the knowledge of the father. He did not destroy those who ate the fruit. He caused those who ate it to come into being and joy in their discovery. And he found them in him, and they found him in them.

Now, as for the illimitable, inconceivable one, that perfect father who made all, the realm of all is in him and the realm of all needs him. He retained in himself their perfection, which he had not given to all. The father was not jealous. What jealousy can be between him and his members? Even if the members of the eternal being had received their perfection, they could not have approached the father's perfection.[5] He retained their perfection in himself, giving it to them as a way to return to him with unique and perfect knowledge. He set all in order, he in whom all are and in whom all stand in need, as one who is not known and wants others to know and love him. For didn't they need knowledge of the father?

Yeshua as Quiet Guide

He became a guide, quiet and at leisure. He appeared in a school and as a teacher spoke the word. Those who thought themselves wise came to test him. But he discredited them as empty-heads. They hated him because they were not wise. After them came the little children, those who possess the knowledge of the father. When they grew strong, they were taught the features of the father's face. They came to know and they were known. They were glorified and they gave glory.

The Living Book in the Hearts of the Little Children

In their hearts the living book of the living was manifest, the book written in the father's thought and mind, which, from before the foundation of all, resides in his incomprehensible nature. No one could take up this book. It was reserved for him who will take it up and be slaughtered. No one could appear among those who believed in salvation as long as that book had not appeared. Compassionate, faithful Jesus was patient in his sufferings until he took up that book, knowing that his death meant life for many. As in a will not yet opened, the fortune of the dead master of the house is concealed, so all that comes from the father was concealed as long as the father of all was invisible. Every realm has its source in him. Jesus appeared and he put on that book. He was nailed to a cross. He affixed the father's edict to the cross.

Oh, such great teaching! He abases himself in death, though he is clothed in eternal life. Having divested himself of these perishable rags, he clothed himself in incorruptibility, which no one could take from him. He entered the empty territory of fears, he passed before those who were stripped by forgetting. For he is both knowledge and perfection, and proclaims what is in the father's heart,[6] and thereby he teaches those who receive his instruction. Those who will learn, the living who inscribed in the book of the living, learn about themselves, receiving instructions from the father, and turn again to him.

The Word of the Father Appears

> Concerning the word,
> his wisdom contemplates it,
> his teaching expresses it,
> his knowledge reveals it,
> his patience is a crown on it,
> his joy accords with it,

his glory exalts it,
his image reveals it,
his rest receives it,
his love embodies it,
his trust embraces it.

Waking Up to Knowledge

What should one think? "I am like the night's shadows and phantoms." When morning comes, one knows that his fear was nothing.

Still, people were ignorant of the father, he whom they did not see. There was terror and confusion and uncertainty and trickery and division. They had many illusions and empty ignorance—as if they were dead asleep and captured by troubling dreams.

The spirit came quickly to a person who awakened. It gave its hand to one lying on the ground. Since he was not on his feet, it stood him up. Knowing the father and having a revelation of his son showed people the way to knowledge. When they saw and listened, he let them take a taste and smell and touch the beloved son. The son appeared, informing them of the father, the illimitable one. He inspired them with the things in his thought while doing his will. Many received the light and turned toward him. He is the shepherd who left behind the ninety-nine sheep that had not strayed and he sought the lost one. He was happy when he found it.

The Father's Sweetness

The father is sweet and his will good. He knows the things that are yours that you may rest in them. By the fruit you know what is yours. The father's children are his aroma. They originated in the grace of his countenance. The father loves his aroma and dispenses it everywhere. When it mixes with matter, it gives the father's aroma to the light, and in his quietness he shows his fragrance to be finer than any sound.

The Father's Paradise

The father is good. He knows his plants since he planted them in his paradise, his place of rest. Paradise is the perfection in the father's thought, and these plants are the words of his meditation. Each word is the work of his will alone and is revealed in his speech. They are the depth of his thought, and the word that came forth made them appear, with mind that utters the word, and grace that is silent. The word[7] was called thought, and these dwelled in it before coming to expression. In this way the word came forth when it pleased the will of him who desired it. The father rests in will. Nothing happens without the father's pleasure, nothing without the father's will.

The Place of the Blessed

All will speak individually of where they have come from and how they were set in the place of rest. They will quickly return and receive from that place, the place where they once stood. They will taste of that place, be fed, and grow. And their own place of rest is their fullness. All the emanations from the father are fullnesses. All his emanations have their roots in the one who made them all grow out of himself. He assigned their destinies. They all were seen to be perfected in their own thought.[8] That place their thought reaches is their root. It makes them soar to the father. They reach his head, which is their rest, and they stay near it and, as it were, touch him and kiss his face.

They are the ones who possess something majestic, some part of immeasurable greatness, as they strain toward the singular and perfect One who is there for them.[9] They do not descend into Hades. They have neither envy nor moaning, nor is death in them. But they rest in him who rests, without weariness or confusion about truth. They are truth, and the father is in them, and they are in the father, since they are perfect, inseparable from him who is good. Such is the place of the blessed. This is their place.

Children like this the father loves.

9

THE SECRET BOOK OF JAMES

The Secret Book of James—also referred to as the Apocryphon of James[1]—is a Christian text with wise sayings and utterances of Jesus, who is in dialogue with his students, particularly Peter and James. It is said in the text that when the twelve students were gathered together, reminiscing about what Jesus had said to them and composing their books, James was doing the same. The sayings incorporated into the Secret Book of James include statements of good fortune and woe, parables and stories, and discourses on being filled and lacking. Many of these sayings recall themes familiar from gnostic sources, and a number of scholars suggest that the Secret Book of James may reflect Valentinian themes. Thus, the text affirms, salvation and the kingdom of heaven may be acquired by being filled with spirit—and by attaining knowledge.

In the selection of the Secret Book of James presented here, the name Yeshua is used for Jesus, Yaakov for James, and Kefa for Cephas (that is, Peter), and the city of Jerusalem is named Yerushalayim.

Yeshua Addresses Kefa and Yaakov

Now, the twelve students were all sitting together, recalling what the savior had said to each of them, whether in a hidden or an open manner, and organizing it in books. I was writing what is in my book. Look, the savior appeared, after he had left us, while we were watching for him.

Five hundred fifty days after he rose from the dead, we said to him, "Did you depart and leave us?"

Yeshua said, "No, but I shall return to the place from which I came. If you want to come with me, come."

They all answered and said, "If you order us, we shall come."

He said, "I tell you the truth, no one will ever enter the kingdom of heaven because I ordered it, but rather because you yourselves are filled. Leave Yaakov and Kefa to me that I may fill them."

When he called the two of them, he took them aside and commanded the rest to keep doing what they were doing.

The savior said, "You have been treated kindly.

Do you not want to be filled?

Your hearts are drunk.

Do you not want to be sober?

You ought to be ashamed.

"From now on, awake or asleep, remember that you have seen the human son and have spoken with him and have listened to him.

"Shame on those who have seen the human son.

"Blessings will be on you who have not seen him, or associated with him, or spoken with him, or listened to anything from him. Yours is life.

"So I tell you: Be filled and leave no space in you empty, or he who is coming will mock you."

Being Filled and Lacking

Then Kefa answered, "Look, three times you have told us, 'Be filled,' but we are filled."

The savior answered and said, "For this reason I have told you, 'Be filled,' that you may not lack. Those who lack will not be saved. To be filled is good and to lack is bad. Yet since it is also good for you to lack but bad for you to be filled, whoever is filled also lacks. So you should lack when you can fill yourselves and be filled when you lack, that you may be able to fill yourselves more. Be filled with spirit but lack in reason, for reason is of the soul. It is soul."[2]

Be Eager for the Word

Then I[3] asked him, "Master, can we prophesy to those who ask us to prophesy to them? There are many who bring a request to us and look to us to hear our pronouncement."

The master said, "First I spoke with you in parables, and you did not understand. Now I am speaking with you openly, and you do not grasp it. Nevertheless, you were for me a parable among parables and a disclosure among things revealed.

"Be eager to be saved without being urged. Rather, be fervent on your own and, if possible, outdo even me, for this is how the father will love you.

"Be eager for the word. The first aspect of the word is faith, the second is love, the third is works, and from these comes life.

"The word is like a grain of wheat. When someone sowed it, he had faith in it, and when it sprouted, he loved it, because he saw many grains instead of just one. And after he worked, he was saved because he prepared it as food and he still kept some out to sow.

"This is also how you can acquire the kingdom of heaven for

yourselves. Unless you acquire it through knowledge, you will not be able to find it."

Shame on You

"You wretches! You poor devils! You pretenders to truth! You falsifiers of knowledge! You sinners against the spirit! Do you still dare to listen when from the beginning you should have been speaking? Do you still dare to sleep when from the beginning you should have been awake so that the kingdom of heaven might receive you? I tell you the truth, it is easier for a holy person to sink into defilement, and for an enlightened person to sink into darkness, than for you to reign—or not to reign.

"I remember your tears, your mourning, and your grief. They are far from us. You who are outside the father's inheritance, weep when you should, mourn, and preach what is good. As is proper, the son is ascending.

"I tell you the truth, if I had been sent to those who would listen to me and had spoken with them, I would never have come down to earth. Now be ashamed.

"Look, I shall be leaving you and go away. I do not want to stay with you any longer just as you yourselves have not wanted this. Follow me quickly. I tell you, for you I came down. You are loved ones. You will bring life to many people. Invoke the father, pray to god frequently, and he will be generous with you."

Know Yourselves

When we heard this, we became sad. But when he saw that we were sad, he said, "I say this to you that you may know yourselves.

"The kingdom of heaven is like a head of grain that sprouted in a field. And when it was ripe, it scattered its seed, and again it filled the field with heads of grain for another year. So with you, be eager to harvest for yourselves a head of the grain of life that you may be filled with the kingdom.

"Do not let the kingdom of heaven become a desert within you. Do not be proud because of the light that enlightens. Rather, act toward yourselves as I myself have toward you. I have put myself under a curse for you to save you."

The Last Word

Kefa responded to these comments and said, "Sometimes you urge us on toward the kingdom of heaven, but at other times you turn us away, master. Sometimes you encourage us, draw us toward faith, and promise us life, but at other times you drive us away from the kingdom of heaven."

The master answered and said to us, "You, through faith and knowledge, have received life. So disregard rejection when you hear it, but when you hear about the promise, be joyful all the more.

"I have spoken my last word to you; I shall depart from you, for a chariot of spirit has carried me up, and from now on I shall strip that I may be clothed."

The Messengers Disperse

When he said this, he left. We knelt down, Kefa and I, and gave thanks and sent our hearts up to heaven. We heard with our ears and saw with our eyes the noise of wars, a trumpet blast, and great turmoil.

When we passed beyond that place, we sent our minds up further. We saw with our eyes and heard with our ears hymns, angelic praises and angelic rejoicing. Heavenly majesties were singing hymns, and we rejoiced too.

Again after this we wished to send our spirits up to the majesty. When we ascended, we were not allowed to see or hear anything. The other students called to us and asked us, "What did you hear from the teacher[4]? What did he tell you? Where did he go?"

We answered them, "He ascended. He gave us his right hand, and promised all of us life. He showed us children coming after us, having commanded us to love them, since we are to be saved for their sakes."

When they heard this, they believed the revelation, but they were angry about those who would be born. Not wishing to give them reason to take offense, I sent each of them to a different location. I myself went up to Yerushalayim, praying that I might acquire a share with the loved ones who are to come.[5]

I pray that the beginning may come from you. This is how I can be saved. They will be enlightened through me, by my faith, and through another's that is better than mine. I wish mine to be the lesser.

Do your best to be like them, and pray that you may acquire a share with them. Beyond what I have said, the savior did not disclose any revelation to us on their behalf. We proclaim a share with those for whom the message was proclaimed, those whom the lord has made his children.

10

THE ROUND DANCE
OF THE CROSS

Contained within the Acts of John is a famous song, with instructions for liturgical dance to accompany the hymn, commonly called the Round Dance of the Cross.[1] The song, which has a gnostic and perhaps even a Valentinian flavor, includes verses sung by Jesus the leader and antiphonal responses of "Amen" from the chorus of students around Jesus. The lines of the verses sung by Jesus employ "I am" statements of a paradoxical sort, and bring to mind the words of the poetic text Thunder. The concluding explanation of the song and the dance elucidates what suffering is and how to transcend it.

The reference to the realm of eight in the Round Dance of the Cross may refer to the Ogdoad, or the Eight, in Valentinian and other gnostic thought, as the realm of the seven planets plus the stars. Note may be taken of the place of the eighth sphere in the text that follows in this collection, Poimandres. The twelfth number in the Round Dance of the Cross may refer to the zodiac or a related twelfth realm. Here, as in other texts, the name Yeshua is given for Jesus.

Yeshua told us to form a circle and hold each other's hands, and he himself stood in the middle, and said, "Respond to me with 'Amen.'"[2]

The Song

So he began by singing a hymn and declaring,
"Glory to you, father."
And we circled around him and responded to him,
"Amen."
"Glory to you, word. Glory to you, grace."
"Amen."
"Glory to you, spirit. Glory to you, holy one. Glory to your
   glory."
"Amen."
"We praise you, father. We give thanks to you, light, in whom
   no darkness is."
"Amen."
"Why we give thanks, I declare:
I will be saved and I will save."
"Amen."
"I will be released and I will release."
"Amen."
"I will be wounded and I will wound."
"Amen."
"I will be born and I will bear."
"Amen."
"I will eat and I will be eaten."
"Amen."
"I will hear and I will be heard."
"Amen."
"I will be kept in mind, being all mind."
"Amen."
"I will be washed and I will wash."
"Amen."

Grace Dances.[3]
"I will play the flute. Dance, everyone."
"Amen."
"I will mourn. Lament, everyone."
"Amen."
"A realm of eight sings with us."
"Amen."
"The twelfth number dances on high."
"Amen."
"The whole universe takes part in dancing."
"Amen."
"Whoever does not dance does not know what happens."
"Amen."

"I will flee and I will stay."
"Amen."
"I will adorn and I will be adorned."
"Amen."
"I will be united and I will unite."
"Amen."
"I have no house and I have houses."
"Amen."
"I have no place and I have places."
"Amen."
"I have no temple and I have temples."
"Amen."
"I am a lamp to you who see me."
"Amen."
"I am a mirror to you who perceive me."
"Amen."
"I am a door to you who knock on me."
"Amen."
"I am a way to you, you passerby."
"Amen."

Understanding the Song

"If you follow my dance,
see yourself in me as I speak,
and if you have seen what I do,
keep silent about my mysteries.

"You who dance, understand what I do,
for yours is the human passion I am to suffer.
You could never understand what you suffer
unless I the word was sent to you by the father.

"You who have seen what I do
have seen me as suffering,
and when you have seen it,
you have not stood firm
but were completely moved.
You were moved to become wise,
and you have me for support.
Rest in me.

"Who I am
you will know when I leave.
What now I am seen to be
I am not.
What I am
you will see when you come.

"If you knew how to suffer
you would be able not to suffer.
Learn about suffering
and you will be able not to suffer.

"What you do not know
I shall teach you.
I am your god,
not the traitor's.
I want holy souls
to be in harmony with me.
Know the word of wisdom.

"Say again with me,
Glory to you, father.
Glory to you, word.
Glory to you, spirit.
Amen.

"If you want to know what I was,
once I mocked everything with the word,
and I was not put to shame at all.
I leaped for joy.
Understand everything,
and when you have understood, declare,
Glory to you, father.
Amen."

11

THE BOOK OF BARUCH

JUSTIN

The Book of Baruch[1] is a Jewish gnostic text, said to have been written by a certain author named Justin, that now exists in a form that is lightly Christianized and hellenized. Baruch is preserved only as a paraphrase in Hippolytus of Rome's Refutation of All Heresies, from which it may be partially recovered. The Book of Baruch recounts the mythic story of the highest god, the Good, along with the male Elohim and the female Edem, and their interactions in the world of humanity. The story of Baruch is a tale of the love of Elohim and Edem, heaven and earth, love that is expressed and is lost, and the mythic tale is related with themes from Genesis as the text explains how the affairs in the divine realm impact human history and the fate of people within this world. The text includes a series of characters from the Hebrew tradition, such as Elohim and Edem, the blessed angel Baruch and the serpentlike angel Naas, and Adam and Eve in the garden of Eden, as well as several figures from Greco-Roman mythological lore.

Here Moshe is the Semitic form of the name used for Moses, Yeshua for Jesus, Yosef for Joseph, and Miryam for Mary, and Natzeret is the city of Nazareth.

Oath of Secrecy

If you would know what eye has not seen nor ear heard
and what has not arisen in the human heart,
and who stands high above all good,
swear to keep the mystery of instruction secret.
Our father, who saw the good perfected in him,
has kept the mysteries of silence secret.
He has sworn and will not waver.
Here is his oath:
"I swear by the one over all, which is the Good,
to keep these mysteries, to tell them to no one,
and not to go from the Good back to the creation."

When you take this oath, you enter the Good
and see what eye has not seen nor ear heard
and what has not arisen in the human heart.
You drink from the living water,
the washing, the spring of living water bubbling up.
And there was a separation of waters from waters,
and the waters below the firmament belong to the evil
    creation.
In them are washed those who are earthly and psychical.
The waters above the firmament belong to the Good
and are alive. The spiritual and the living are washed in them
as Elohim was after the washing. He did not waver.

The Myth of the Creators

There were three ungenerated principles
governing the cosmos: two male and one female.
One of the male principles is called the Good,

and it alone carries that epithet
and knows everything ahead of time.
The other male principle is named father of all things
begotten in the world, has no forethought,
and he is unknown and invisible.
The female is angry.
She knows nothing ahead of time
and she has two minds and two bodies. As in Herodotos's
    myth,
she is a virgin above and a viper below.[2]
She is called both Edem[3] and Israel.
These are the principles of the cosmos,
the roots and pools from which all sprang,
and nothing else was in the world.

When the father knowing nothing beforehand
saw that half-virgin Edem, he burned for her,
and he the father is called Elohim,[4]
and Edem burned equally for Elohim. Their desire
drew them to a single union of love.
From this coupling the father seeded twelve angels
for himself through Edem.
The paternal angels are Michael, Amen, Baruch, Gabriel,
    Esaddaeus,   .[5]
The maternal angels are Babel, Achamoth, Naas, Bel, Belias,
    Satan,
Sael, Adonaios, Kauithan, Pharaoth, Karkamenos, and
   . Lathen.
Of these twenty-four the paternal ones side
with the father and obey his will in everything,
and the maternal ones hear their mother, Edem.
Their common domain is paradise,
about which Moshe tells us,
"God planted paradise east of Eden,"

before the face of Edem, and therefore
she always looks at paradise, her angels.

The angels of paradise are allegorically called trees,
and the tree of life is the third paternal angel,
and his name is Baruch,
while the tree of the knowledge of good and evil
is the third maternal angel, and he is Naas.
Moshe spoke these things covertly
because not everyone can hold the truth.

The Creation of Adam and Eve

After paradise came into being through the love
of Elohim and Edem,
the angels of Elohim took some of the best earth
(not from the bestial, naked part of Edem
but from her upper, civilized regions)
and from that good earth they made man,
but from the bestial land came wild beasts and creatures.

They made man a symbol of their union and love
and planted some of their powers in him.
Edem provided the soul and Elohim the spirit.
The man Adam was a seal and memory of their love,
an eternal symbol of the wedding of Edem and Elohim.
And, as Moshe wrote, Eve was image and symbol,
and the seal of Edem preserved forever.
Edem set the soul in Eve and Elohim the spirit.

And they were given commandments:
"Be fruitful and multiply and subdue the earth."
Edem gave away all her power to Elohim,

like a marriage dowry, and till this day,
in imitation of that first marriage,
a woman comes to her husband with a dowry,
obeying a holy and hereditary law
that Edem carried out toward Elohim.

The Angels Are Divided

When, according to Moshe, everything was created
including heaven and earth and all therein,
the twelve angels of the mother were divided
into four principles, and each quadrant is called
a river: Pishon, Gihon, Tigris, and Euphrates.
Huddled in these four parts, the twelve angels
circle around and govern the cosmos.
Their authority over the world comes from Edem.
They are not forever in the same region,
but as in a circular chorus they move
from place to place at fixed intervals and periods
according to their assignments.
When the angels of Pishon rule a region,
then famine, distress, and tribulation
foul that segment of the earth,
for their criterion for ruling is avarice.
And in all regions come bad times and disease
according to each power and nature.
There is a torrent of evil pouring out
like the rivers, and constantly around the world
Edem's will controls every quadrant.

Elohim's Ascent

The necessity of evil has this circumstance:
when Elohim and Edem in mutual love made the cosmos,
Elohim chose to rise to the highest part of heaven
to see if their creation lacked any elements.
He took his angels with him and rose, as was his nature,
and he abandoned Edem below,
who, being earth, declined to follow her husband upward.
When Elohim reached the upper border of heaven,
he saw a light stronger than the sun he created,
and he said, "Open the gates for me to enter
and to acknowledge the lord.
I had thought I was the lord!"

He heard a voice out of the light, saying,
"This is the lord's gate. The just pass through it."
The gate was immediately opened,
and the father, without his angels, went into the Good
and saw what eye has not seen or ear heard
and what has not arisen in the human heart.
The Good said to him, "Sit down at my right hand."
The father said to the Good,
"Let me destroy the cosmos I made.
My spirit is imprisoned among people.
I want to take it back."

Then the Good told him, "Nothing that comes
from me can be evil. In your companion love
you and Edem made the world. Let Edem keep the creation
as long as she wishes, but you must stay with me."

Edem's Response

Then Edem knew she was abandoned by Elohim
and sorrowfully began to gather angels around her
and adorn herself brightly to arouse his return.
But under the Good's control Elohim no longer
descended to Edem. Then Edem commanded Babel,
which here means the goddess Aphrodite,
to incite fornication and divorce among people,
so that as she was separated from Elohim
the spirit of Elohim in people might feel affliction
and be tormented and suffer like her, Edem,
his abandoned wife. And Edem gave grand authority
to Naas, her third angel, to torture the spirit
of Elohim in people with all possible tortures
so through that spirit Elohim might himself
be tortured—he who had abandoned Edem
in cold violation of their covenant.

Elohim Sends Down His Angel Baruch

When the father Elohim saw these things,
he sent down Baruch, his own third angel,
to comfort the spirit living in all people.
When Baruch came he stood among the angels
of Edem, in the midst of paradise. Paradise
was the angels among whom he stood,
and he commanded the people "to eat from
every tree in paradise, except from the tree
of the knowledge of good and evil,"
which tree is Naas. They could obey
the other eleven angels of Edem,

for though they have passions, they do not disobey
the commandment. But Naas disobeyed.
He approached Eve and seduced her
and debauched her, which is a transgression,
and he approached Adam and played with him
as a boy, which is a transgression.
So adultery and pederasty were born.
Since then evil and good have ruled people.
It began from a single source. When the father
ascended to the Good, he showed the way
for those who wish to rise, and by leaving Edem
he began the evil for his spirit in people.

Baruch Searches for a Savior

Baruch went to Moshe and through him spoke
to the children of Israel to turn them back to the Good,
but Edem's third angel Naas barred his way.
Through the soul Edem gave him and Moshe
and all people, Naas expunged Baruch's orders
and only Naas's commandments were heard,
and so soul was set against spirit
and spirit set against soul.
The soul is Edem while the spirit is Elohim,
and each is in both man and woman.

Then Baruch was sent down to the prophets
so that the spirit living in people might hear
and flee from Edem and her corrupt creation
as once father Elohim fled. But Naas, using
his old tactics, dragged the father's spirit down
into the soul of people he seduced, who scorned
Baruch's words in Elohim's commandments.

Then Baruch chose a prophet from the uncircumcised,
Herakles, and sent him to subdue the twelve angels
of Edem, and free the father from the twelve evil
angels of the creation. These are the twelve labors
in which Herakles contended, from first to last,
with the lion, the hydra, the boar, and the rest.
And they are names of nations given to them
from the power of the maternal angels.
Just when he seemed victorious, Omphale,
who is Babel or Aphrodite, attacked him
and seduced him and took away his strength
and Baruch's commandments ordered by Elohim,
and then she wrapped him in her own robe,
the power of Edem, the power from below.
Herakles' prophecies and work were nothing.

Baruch Finds Yeshua

Finally, "in the days of King Herod,"
Baruch was sent once more by Elohim
and he came to Natzeret and found Yeshua,
son of Yosef and Miryam, feeding sheep,
a boy of twelve, and he told him everything
that had happened from the beginning,
from Edem and Elohim and all that will be.
He said, "All the prophets before you
were seduced, but Yeshua, earthly son,
try not to be seduced, and preach the word
to people and tell them about the father
and the Good, and ascend to the Good
and sit with Elohim, father of us all."

Yeshua's Crucifixion and Ascent

And Yeshua obeyed the angel. He said,
"Lord, I will do all things." He affirmed this.
Naas wanted to seduce him too, but he
could not. Yeshua kept faith with Baruch.
Then Naas was enraged because he could not
seduce him, and he had him crucified.
Yeshua left his body to Edem by the tree
and ascended to the Good. He said to her,
"Woman, here is your son." He left
his soul and earthly body, but his spirit
he placed in the hands of the father
and then he ascended to the Good.

Allegorical Interpretations

The Good is Priapos, who created before
anything was. He is called Priapos
because he made everything. So in temples
everywhere he is honored by all creation.
On the roads he walks carrying fruit,
fruits of creation, whose cause he was,
since he created before anything was.

Now, when you hear that the swan lay on Leda
and produced a child from her,
the swan is Elohim and Leda is Edem.

When they say that the eagle came upon Ganymede,
the eagle is Naas and Ganymede is Adam.

When you hear one say that gold came upon Danae
and produced a child from her,
the gold is Elohim and Danae is Edem.

In this way these tales are interpreted
comparing them to similar myths.

When the prophets say, "Hear, heaven,
and listen, earth, the lord has spoken,"
the spirit of Elohim in people is heaven,
and soul living with the spirit in people is earth.
The lord is Baruch, and Israel Edem,
and Elohim's wife is called Edem and Israel.
"Israel did not know me." And if she[6] had known
that I[7] am with the Good, she would not
have tortured the spirit that lives in people
because of the ignorance of the father.
When the prophet is said to take a woman
for himself to fornicate because "the earth has fornicated
behind the lord," even as Edem behind Elohim,
in these words the prophet clearly tells the whole mystery,
but because of Naas's wickedness he is unheard.

12

THE SONG OF THE PEARL

The Song of the Pearl[1] is a narrative poem about a prince's quest for a pearl. The song emerges in the Syrian religious tradition, and it is presented in the Acts of Thomas as a hymn uttered by the apostle Thomas. In song the princely speaker recalls how he was sent from the east to find a pearl in Egypt, but while he is there, he encounters a serpent and falls into a deep sleep. The prince is awakened by the words of a letter from home, and he arises, puts on a garment of gnosis, and returns to the eastern kingdom. The Song of the Pearl tells a story of a princely journey, but it is also a tale of gnosis and salvation, of sleeping in error and awakening to light, of a quest not only for a pearl but for the spiritual benefit of possessing the pearl—a return to the light.

~

Dressing for the Journey

> When I was a little child living
> in my father's palace in his kingdom,
> happy in the glories and riches
> of my family that nurtured me,

my parents gave me supplies
and sent me out on a mission
from our home in the east.
From their treasure house
they made up a cargo for me.
It was big though light enough
so I could carry it myself,
holding gold from the highest houses
and silver of Gazzak the Great
and rubies of India
and opals from the land of Kushan,
and they girded me with adamant
that can crush iron.
They took off my bright robe of glory,
which they had made for me out of love,
and took away my purple toga,
which was woven to fit my stature.
They made a covenant with me
and wrote it in my heart so I would not forget:
"When you go down into Egypt
and bring back the one pearl
that lies in the middle of the sea
and is guarded by the snorting serpent,
you will again put on your robe of glory
and your toga over it,
and with your brother, our next in rank,
you will be heir in our kingdom."

The Dragon and the Deep Sleep

I left the east and traveled down
to Egypt with my two royal guides,
since the way was dangerous and harsh

and I was very young to walk alone.
I crossed the borders of Maishan,
the gathering place of merchants of the east,
came into the land of the Babylonians,[2]
and entered the walls of Sarbug.
When I went down into Egypt,
my companions left me.
I went straight to the serpent
and settled close by him in an inn,
waiting for him to sleep
so I could take my pearl from him.
Since I was alone,
I was a stranger to others in the inn,
yet I saw one of my own people there,
a nobleman from the east,
young, handsome, lovable,
a son of kings—an anointed one,
and he came and was close to me.
And I made him my confidant
with whom I shared my mission.
I warned him against the Egyptians
and of contact with the unclean ones.
Then I put on a robe like theirs,
lest they suspect me as an outsider
who had come to steal the pearl,
lest they arouse the serpent against me.
Somehow they learned I was not
their countryman, dealt with me cunningly,
and gave me their food to eat.
I fell into a deep sleep.
I forgot that I was a son of kings
and served their king.
I forgot the pearl
for which my parents had sent me.

Through the heaviness of their food
I fell into a deep sleep.

"Remember the Pearl"

When all these things happened
my parents knew and grieved for me.
It was proclaimed in our kingdom
that all should come to our gate.
And the kings and princes of Parthia
and all the nobles of the east
wove a plan on my behalf
so I would not be left in Egypt.
And they wrote me a letter
and every noble signed it with his name:
"From your father, the king of kings,
and your mother, the mistress of the east,
and from your brother, our next in rank,
and to you, our son in Egypt, peace!
Awake and rise from your sleep
and hear the words of our letter!
Remember that you are a son of kings
and see the slavery of your life.
Remember the pearl
for which you were sent into Egypt!
Remember your robe of glory
and your splendid mantle, which you may wear
when your name is called in the book of life,
when it is read in the book of heroes,
when you and your brother inherit our
    kingdom."

The Bird of Speech

And serving as messenger,
the letter was a letter sealed by the king
with his right hand
against the evil children of Babylon
and the savage demons of the Sarbug labyrinth.
It rose up in the form of an eagle,
the king of all winged fowl;
it flew and alighted beside me
and became speech.
At its voice and the sound of its rustling
I awoke and rose from my sleep.
I took it, kissed it, broke its seal, and read.
And the words written on my heart
were in the letter for me to read.
I remembered that I was the son of kings
and my free soul longed for its own kind.
I remembered the pearl
for which I was sent down into Egypt,
and I began to enchant
the terrible and snorting serpent.
I charmed him into sleep
by calling the name of my father over him
and of my mother, the queen of the east.
I seized the pearl
and turned to carry it to my father.
Those filthy and impure garments
I stripped off, leaving them in the fields,
and went straight on my way
into the light of our homeland in the east.

The Letter's Voice

On my way the letter that awakened me
was lying like a woman on the road.[3]
And as she had awakened me with her voice,
so she guided me with her light
as if she were an oracle.
She was written on Chinese silk
and shone before me in her own form.
Her voice soothed my fear
and its love urged me on.
I hurried past the labyrinth walls of Sarbug
and Babylon on the left
and came to Maishan, the haven of merchants,
perched over the coast of the sea.
My robe of glory that I had taken off
and the toga over it were sent by my parents
from the heights of Hyrcania.
They were in the hands of treasurers
to whom they were committed
because of their faith,
and I had forgotten the robe's splendor,
for as a child I had left it
in my father's house.

The Garment of Gnosis

As I gazed on it, suddenly the garment
like a mirror reflected me,
and I saw myself apart
as two entities in one form.
The treasurers had brought me one robe,

yet in two halves I saw one shape
with one kingly seal.
They gave me wealth,
and the bright embroidered robe
was colored with gold and beryls,
with rubies and opals,
and sardonyxes of many colors
were fastened to it in its high home.
All its seams were fastened
with stones of adamant,
and the image of the king of kings
was embroidered on it
as it rippled with sapphires
of many colors.
I saw it quiver all over,
moving with gnosis, in a pulsing knowledge,
and as it prepared to speak
it moved toward me,
murmuring the sound of its songs.
It descended and said,
"I am the one who acted for him.
For him I was brought up in my father's house.
I saw myself growing in stature
in harmony with his labors."

The Toga and the Pearl

With regal movements
the robe was spreading toward me,
urging me to take it,
and love urged me to receive it,
and I stretched forth and received it
and put on the beauty of its hues.

I cast my toga of brilliant colors
all around me.
Therein I clothed myself and ascended
to the gate of salutation and adoration.
I bowed my head and adored
the majesty of my father, who sent it to me.
I had fulfilled his commands
and he fulfilled what he had promised.
At the gate of his princes
I mingled with his nobles.
He was happy through me and received me,
and I was with him in his kingdom,
and his slaves praised him resoundingly.
He promised me that I would journey soon
with him to the gate of the king of kings,
and with my gifts and my pearl
I would appear with him before our king.

13

THE SONGS OF SOLOMON

The Songs of Solomon, or the Odes of Solomon,[1] also derive from the Syrian religious heritage, and a few of the wisdom poems in this rich poetic collection are added here. While scholars disagree about how gnostic the Songs of Solomon are, their haunting beauty and mystical imagery contribute to an appreciation of the central place of wisdom and knowledge in the world of Jewish, Christian, and gnostic mysticism.

Song 15

> As the sun is joy to those who seek daybreak, my joy is
>   the lord.
> He is my sun and his rays have lifted me up
> and chased all darkness from my face.
> I have acquired eyes and heard his truth.
> I have acquired knowledge, and he made me happy.
> I left the way of error, went to him, and he saved me.
> According to his bounty, he gave me;
> according to his beauty, he made me.

I found purity through his name.
I shed corruption through his grace.
Death has died before my countenance.
Hell is abolished by my word.
A deathless life appears in the land of the lord,
known to those with belief, and lasts unceasingly.

Song 21

I raised my arms high to the grace of the lord,
for he cast off my bonds.
My helper had raised me to his grace and salvation.
I discarded darkness
and dressed in the clothing of light.
My soul acquired a body free from sorrow,
free from torture and mutilation.
The lord's thought restored me.
I fed on his incorruptible fellowship.
In the light he raised me.
I went to him, near him,
praising and shouting his name.
He made my heart flood into my mouth.
He made it shine on my lips.
On my face the exultation of the lord grew.
My praise exploded.

Song 35

The dew of the lord rinsed me with silence
and a cloud of peace rose over my head,
guarding me.
It became my salvation.

Everybody quivered in horror.
They issued smoke and judgment
but I was silent, near my lord,
who was more than shadow, more than foundation.

He carried me like a child by its mother.
He gave me milk, his dew,
and I grew in his bounty
and rested in his perfection.
I spread my hands out
as my soul pointed to the firmament
and I slipped upward to him
who redeemed me.

14

POIMANDRES

The Hermetic text entitled Poimandres[1] is a leading text in the tradition of the revelations of knowledge and wisdom attributed to Hermes Trismegistos, thrice-greatest Hermes. These Hermetic revelations make up a collection called the Corpus Hermeticum, and the present text is the first document in that collection. In this text the figure of Poimandres, whose name may mean "shepherd of man," enters into a dialogue with a speaker who is in search of knowledge. Poimandres states that he is the mind of absolute power and the first god, and he proceeds to provide revelatory insights into the origin of the cosmos, the birth of the primal human, and the salvation of the soul. What is supremely good for those who possess gnosis, Poimandres concludes, is to ascend to the heights of enlightenment and become divine, and that is the goal for the speaker in the dialogue and anyone who may choose to be a devout reader of Poimandres.

Poimandres Appears

Once when I began to think about the things that are, and my thoughts soared exceedingly high, and my bodily senses were held down by sleep like people weighed down by overeating and weariness, I thought I saw a being of vast and boundless magnitude coming toward me, who called me by name, and said, "What do you wish to hear and see, to learn and know?"

"Who are you?" I said.

"I am Poimandres," he said, "the mind of absolute power. I know what you want and I am with you everywhere."

"I want to learn about the things that are, their nature, and to know god," I replied. "How I want to hear!"

He said, "Keep in mind what you wish to learn and I will teach you."

The Vision of Creation

With these words he changed his form, and in a flash everything opened before me and I saw an unbounded vista. All was light, a soothing and happy light. And as I gazed I was entranced. But soon a stark and terrifying darkness descended gradually like a coiled snake, and I saw the darkness turn into a watery substance, unspeakably agitated, giving off smoke as from fire, emitting an indescribable sound of lamentation. And after that an inarticulate cry like the voice of fire.

Out of the light a holy word[2] descended upon the watery substance, and I thought this word the voice of light; and unmingled fire leaped out of the watery substance and soared upward. The fire was quick and violent, and the air, being light, followed the breath[3] as it rose from earth and water to the fire, so that the breath seemed suspended from the fire. But the earth and water remained intermingled, and the earth could not be seen apart from the water. All these elements were kept in audible motion by the breath of the word hovering above them.

Poimandres Is Light and Mind

Then Poimandres asked me, "Do you understand what that vision means?"

"I will understand," I said.

"I am that light," he said, "and I am the mind, the first god, who existed before the watery substance appeared out of the darkness. And the luminous word that issued from the mind is the son of god."

"In what way?"

"Understand that what sees and hears inside you is the word of the lord, its son, but the mind is god the father. And they are not divided one from the other, for they are united by life."

"Thank you," I said.

"But think about the light, and understand it."

Where Everything Comes From

Having said this, he gazed intently at me for a long time, and I trembled at his aspect. When I raised my head I saw in my mind the light, consisting of innumerable powers, which had become a limitless cosmos, and the fire, contained by a mighty power, was held in place. This is what I saw and understood from the words of Poimandres.

I was amazed, and he spoke to me again. "You have seen in your mind the archetypal form, infinite and prior to the beginning."

"But where do the elements of nature come from?" I asked.

"From god's will, which received the word, and saw and imitated the beautiful world. The watery substance of nature received the word and made itself into an orderly world from its diverse elements, and a brood of living creatures came forth.

Another Mind, the Demiurge

"And the first mind, being both male and female, both life and light, conceived through the word another mind, the demiurge, and this second mind of fire and breath fashioned seven rulers, who encompass within their orbits the world perceived by the senses. Their government is called destiny.

"Suddenly, the word of god leaped out of the downward-moving elements of nature to the pure body of heaven and was united with the mind of the demiurge. For the word was of one substance with the mind. And the lower elements of nature were left wordless, that is, without reason, and became mere matter.

"Now the demiurge-mind worked together with the word to encompass the spheres of the rulers and to whirl them with thunderous speed, with no fixed beginning or determined end, since their revolutions begin where they end. And according to the mind's will, the lower elements of nature became animals devoid of reason, for they did not have the word. And the air brought forth winged creatures, and the water brought forth fish, and by then earth and water were separated from each other according to the will of the mind. And earth brought forth four-footed creatures and creeping things and wild and tame beasts.

Mind, Father of All, Gives Birth to a Primal Human

"But mind, the father of all, who is life and light, gave birth to a human being like himself. And he loved him as his own child, for he was very beautiful, bearing the likeness of his father. And god was very pleased with his own beauty in the primal person[4] and delivered to him all that he had created.

"And the primal person took station in the highest sphere of heaven and observed the things made by its author, his brother the demiurge, who ruled over the region of fire. Now that the human had seen those things made in fire, he wished to create things of his own. And his father permitted him to do so. And since the rulers loved him too, each gave him a share of his own nature.

"When the human learned their characteristics, he wished to break through the bounding orbits of the rulers and to share the power of him who rules over the fire.

The Human Descends into the World of Nature

"Then the primal person, who possessed all authority over the world of mortal creatures and irrational animals, leaned down through the harmony and, having broken the vault, showed lower nature the beautiful form of god. When nature saw the beautiful form of god, it smiled on the human with love, for it had seen the wondrous beauty of the human reflected in the water and its shadow on the earth. And the human too, on seeing this form, a form similar to his own reflected in the water, loved it and wanted to live in it. And his wish was immediately realized, and he began to inhabit a form devoid of reason. And nature received its loved one, embraced him, and they mingled, for they were lovers.

Humankind Is Mortal and Immortal

"And this is why the human, of all creatures on the earth, is twofold: mortal in his body but immortal through the eternal human. Though he is immortal and has power over all things, he also suffers mortality, since he is subject to destiny. Though above the world of the spheres, he is a slave of destiny. Though he is male and female,[5] being born of a father who contains male and female, and is sleepless as his father is sleepless, he is vanquished by love and oblivion."

Seven Earthly Humans Are Born

And after this I said, "O mind, tell me the rest. I too love your teaching."

And Poimandres answered, "Here is the mystery that has been hidden until this day. Nature, intimately mingled with the primal person, produced a most wondrous miracle. The human had in himself the world of spheres of the seven rulers, which, as I told you, was made of fire and air. Nature immediately made seven humans corresponding to the natures of the seven rulers, and they were androgynous and sublime."

Then I said, "O Poimandres, a powerful desire has seized me and I want to hear more. Do not stop."

"Silence," Poimandres replied. "I have not yet finished with the first discourse."

"See, I am silent," I said.

"These seven humans were born as follows: nature brought forth their bodies. Earth was the female element, water the generative male element; from fire came their nature, from ether their spirit. Nature brought forth their bodies in human likeness. And humankind, which was formed of life and light, became soul and mind: soul from life and mind from light. And all creatures in the world of senses remained that way until the end of an era.

Male and Female Are Created

"Now I will tell you what you long to hear. When that era was completed, the bond uniting all things was loosened by god's will.

All living creatures, being androgynous, were suddenly divided into two, and the primal person became at once male and female. God immediately spoke a holy word: 'Increase and multiply, all you creatures and creations. And let humankind, being with a mind, recognize itself as immortal and know that the cause of death is eros.'

"And when god said this, his providence,[6] by means of destiny and the world of spheres, brought male and female into union and established generations. And all creatures multiplied according to their kind. And whoever recognized himself attained that good that is supreme, while whoever was led astray by desire, by love for the body, will wander in the darkness of the world of senses and suffer death."

Life and Death

"But what kind of sin do the ignorant commit that they should be deprived of immortality?" I asked.

"You do not seem to have thought about what I told you. Did I not tell you to pay attention?"

"I understand and remember, and at the same time I thank you."

"If you understand, tell me why those who are ignorant deserve death."

"Because the material body has its source in the abhorrent darkness, from which came the watery substance of which the body is composed in the sensible world, and from this body death slakes its thirst."

"You have understood correctly. But why is it, as the word of god has it, that whoever recognizes and knows himself enters into the good?"

I answered, "Because the father of all consists of light and life, and from him human beings were born."

"You are right. Light and life are god and father, out of which humans came. And if you learn that you are also made of light and life, you will return to light and life." These things Poimandres said.

The Place of the Mind Among the Godly and Godless

"But tell me," I said, "how I shall come into life, for god told me, 'Let the thinking person know himself.' Don't all people have a mind?"

"Do not speak that way, for I, mind, am present to the holy and good and pure and merciful, and my presence is a help to them, and all at once they recognize everything and win the mercy of loving god, and thank him and praise him and sing hymns to him, and turn to him with devotion. And before they abandon the body to death, they loathe the bodily senses, since they know how they work. I, the mind, will not allow the workings of the body to attain their purpose. As a guardian of the gates, I bar the way to evil and shameful energies. I cut off their strategies.

"And I am far removed from those who are foolish and evil and sly and envious and covetous and murderous and godless. I yield place to the avenging demon who visits such a person with the sharpness of fire, piercing his senses and driving him to further lawlessness so that he may incur greater punishment. Never ceasing his dark struggle, and giving in to boundless appetite, he inflicts upon himself greater torment and hotter fire."

The Ascent of the Soul through Seven Zones

"Mind, you have instructed me well in all things. But tell me more about the ascent. How shall I come to life?"

At this Poimandres said, "First, with the dissolution of your material body, you yield your character to the demon. Your image vanishes. The bodily senses return to their own sources, becoming part of the cosmos, and, combined in new ways, do other work. And anger and desire enter thoughtless nature.

"And then man rises into the harmony, the world of the spheres. In the first zone he leaves behind the force to grow and decrease, in the second the machinations of evil, in the third the guile of lust, in the fourth his domineering arrogance, in the fifth his unholy daring and rashness, in the sixth his striving for wealth by evil means, and in the seventh zone the malicious lie: all rendered powerless.

Entering the Eighth and Becoming Divine

"Then, stripped naked by the force of the harmony, he enters the eighth sphere of the fixed stars, and possessing his own energy he remains there with others, singing hymns to the father. And the others are happy at his coming. Resembling those who live there, he hears the powers who have their place in the substance of the eighth sphere and who sing to god with a special voice. They move in order up to the father. They surrender to the powers, and become the powers, and are in god. This is the good, the aim of those who have gnosis: to become god.

"Why then do you hesitate? Now that you have received everything from me, why not make yourself a guide to the worthy so that people may be saved by god through you?" And, having said these things, Poimandres before my eyes mingled with the powers.

Going Forth to Preach

I thanked and blessed the father of all, and was sent forth, empowered and instructed concerning the nature of all and with a supreme vision. And I began to preach to the people of beauty, of piety and gnosis: "O people born of the earth, given over to drunkenness and sleep and ignorance of god, end your drunkenness and unreasoning sleep."

When they heard this, they gathered around me. I said, "Why have you accepted death when you have been given the power to enjoy immortality? Change your ways, you who walk with error and keep company with ignorance. Free yourself of darkness and seize the light. Abandon corruption and receive immortality."

And some of them mocked me and left me, for they had given themselves to death. But others begged me to teach them, and they threw themselves at my feet. I raised them up and became a guide to people, teaching them the word and how they might be saved. And I sowed words of wisdom in them, and they were nourished with ambrosial water. When evening came and the rays of sun began to fade, I called on them to thank god. And when they completed the thanksgiving, each sought his or her own bed.

I recorded the beneficence of Poimandres, and how my hopes had been fulfilled. For the body's sleep became the soul's awakening, the closing of my eyes the true vision, my silence pregnant with the good, and my words the expression of good things. And all this happened to me, since I had received it from my mind, that is, from Poimandres, the word and mind of absolute sovereignty. I became god-inspired, god-minded, and came with the truth.

Praise to God the Father

So with all my soul and strength I praise god the father:

> Holy is god the father of all, who precedes all beginnings.
> Holy is god, whose will is accomplished by his own powers.
> Holy is god, who wishes to be known and is known to those
> who are his own.
> You are holy, who by your word made all things that are.
> You are holy, who have become the image of all nature.
> You are holy, who are not formed by nature.
> You are holy, who are stronger than all domination.
> You are holy, who are greater than all eminence.
> You are holy, who are superior to all praise.

Accept the pure offering of words from a soul and heart that rise to you, unnamable, ineffable, whom only silence calls!

I beg you, let me not be removed from gnosis, which is our nature. Fill me with strength, and with your grace let me bring light to those of my race who are in ignorance, to my brothers and sisters, sons and daughters. Therefore I believe and bear witness. I go to life and to light.

Father, bless you. Your child wishes to share the holy salvation you confer through your total authority.

15

THE GINZA

The Ginza[1] is the holy book of the Mandaeans, the gnostics who come from the marshes of southern Iraq and Iran and now may be found in communities throughout the world. The word Ginza means "treasure," and the text contains a rich assemblage of mythological, theological, and ritual materials. The brief selections from the Ginza provided here describe Ptahil, the creator god, working on Adam, while Manda dHayye, the Mandaean messenger of light, whose name means "knowledge of life," cares for the soul and the life of the human. In the Ginza, the term Tibil indicates the physical world, Adakas Ziwa the radiant figure of Adam, and Ruha the fallen spirit of wisdom. The reference to the Jordan is reflective of the baptismal interests of the Mandaeans.

Creating Adam and Giving Him a Soul

After the angel Ptahil came, he said to the planets, "Let us create Adam and make him king of the world." They made Adam and laid him on the ground, but he had no soul.

Ptahil wrapped Adam in his clean turban.
He wrapped him in his robe.
The light being quickly descended, and his helpers all went
    down with him.
His helpers who went down are men in charge of souls.
When they reached the Tibil, which is the world and where
    his bodily torso is,
when Ptahil wanted to cast soul into his body,
I, Manda dHayye, removed the soul from his pocket.
When Ptahil lifted Adam up, I raised his bones.
When he laid his hands on him, I made him breathe the
    fragrance of life.
His body filled with marrow,
and the radiance of life spoke in him.
When the radiance of life spoke in him,
he opened the eyes of his bodily torso.
When the radiance of life spoke in him,
Adakas Ziwa, the radiant Adam, rose to his place.

Manda dHayye, Messenger of Light

I led Adam up to his place.
I led Adam up to his place, the house of powerful life,
the house where the great life is on his throne.
I came and found the wicked, all of them sitting there,
and while they were sitting there
I spread witchcraft and magic around the soul,
and the wicked wanted to chop the soul into tiny parts.
I saw them and I shone in my pure garments.
I appeared to Ptahil Uthra, who howled and wept.
He howled and wept over what he had done.
I appeared to Ruha, the seductive mother of planets and evil
    creatures,

who seduces the worlds.
I showed her the great mystery that subdues rebels.
I showed her the great mystery, but she was blind and didn't
see it.
I showed her a second mystery.
Then I threw a camel bridle on her and showed her a third
mystery
and with a blow I split her head open.

The Light Being of Life Rewards Adam

For what Adam had done the light being of life was kind,
the father of light was full of kindness to him
and commanded a building be erected for him
and commanded a planting be planted for him.
He commanded a Jordan river be prepared for him
so at the ripe instant when his measure was full,
he would ascend and inhabit his building and inhabit
the place of light
with Adakas Ziwa his father,
and become a light being in the place of light.

SOUL SONGS

Adam Enveloped in Sleep

I am enveloped in sleep
in a robe without error,
in a robe without error
in which nothing lacks.
Life knew about me:
Adam asleep. I woke.

The soul took my hand.
Light hurled me into darkness,
darkness filled with light.
On the day the light rises
darkness will go to its cave.
She came to clouds of light,
going to the place of light.

The Savior Talks to the Soul

Soul, if you hear what I say
and do not oppose my word,
for you I will throw a bridge
over the great sea.
For you I will lay a dam
and guide you to the watchtower
where the rebels hold out.
I will guide you past the fire
and smoke touching the sky.
I will take you past the double pits
where Ruha has dug her way.
And over that high mountain
I will smooth the path for you.
In this wall, this wall of iron,
I will hack a breach for you,
hug you with all my strength,
and take you to the place of light.

Loving Life, Performing Good Deeds

Loving life, I let Manda dHayye,
the messenger of light,

calm my innermost thought.
Late Saturday evening
and before the good Sunday,
I stuffed alms in my pocket
and went to the temple gate.
I piled alms and bread
on the common plate.
I found an orphan. I fed him.
I found a widow. I filled her pocket.
I found a naked man
and gave him a garment
for his nakedness.
I found a prisoner and found a way
to free him to his village.

16

SONGS FROM THE MANDAEAN LITURGY

The Songs from the Mandaean Liturgy[1] given here represent examples taken from the ritual texts of the Mandaean gnostics. These texts sing of a poor man who is a stranger in this world, a kind being who offers light, and a letter that communicates life. The last song recommends, "Be like wine jars."

~

SONG OF THE POOR MAN

A Poor Man Taken Far

> I am a poor man from the fruit.
> They took me from far away. I am far.
> I am a poor man whom life spoke to.
> I am far. The light beings took me away.
> They carried me here from the good
> to where the wicked live.
> They installed me in the world of the wicked
> where all is malice and fire.

I didn't ask for it. I didn't want to come
to this awful place.
By my strength and light I suffer through
this misery. By illumination and praise.
I remain a stranger in their world.
I stand among the wicked like a child without a father.
Like a fatherless child, an untended fruit.
I hear the voice of the seven planets.
They whisper. They say among themselves,
"Where does this alien come from?
He doesn't speak like us."
I didn't listen to their speech raging against me.

The Kindly Light Being

Life heard my cry and sent an angel,
a kindly light being who was prepared for me.
He told me in a pure voice
as light beings speak in the house of perfection.
He said, "Poor man, don't be alarmed or fearful.
Don't say, 'I am utterly alone.'
For you we spread the firmament above.
For you we spread the firmament above and made dry land.
We made dry land,
and solid land came and stood in the water.
For you the sun came,
for you the moon came into the firmament,
for you, poor one, the seven planets
and twelve creatures of the zodiac were set in orbit.
Radiance sits at your right hand
and glittering light on your left.
Be strong in your seed until you are fulfilled.
I will bring you a lovely shawl of light,

abundant and boundless.
You will sit in your own heavenly place."

A Letter Looped around One's Neck

Here is a sealed letter
leaving the world,
a letter written with truth
and marked with the seal
of mighty life.
Perfect ones wrote it,
and believers insured it.
They looped it around
the soul's neck
and sent it to the gate
of life. The soul wisely
used her finger
to mark the open letter.

Be Like Wine Jars

You of my blood, speak the truth.
Close your lying lips.
Don't be a pomegranate whose outer face is fresh.
Its outer face is fresh, but inside it is full
of rotting corn seed.
Be like wine jars filled with redolent wine.
Their outer shells are clay and pitch,
but inside is redolent wine.
The message of life shouts. Ears of my chosen,
come and hear me.

17

THE COPTIC MANICHAEAN SONGBOOK

Manichaeism was one of the major religions of the world from the time of late antiquity and thereafter. Founded by the Iranian prophet Mani, this dynamic religious tradition incorporated Christian, Zoroastrian, Buddhist, and gnostic themes into its theology and practice. Manichaean religion attained nearly universal proportions, and it spread throughout southern Europe, northern Africa, the Middle East, and central and eastern Asia. The textual tradition of Manichaean religion is especially significant, and among the most impressive texts within Manichaean literature are the songs and hymns of the Coptic Manichaean Songbook.[1] The songs selected for inclusion in the present collection celebrate the liberation of one who is beautiful but oppressed in the world, and the return of the light below to the glory of the light above. The soul that sleeps awakens with the dawn, and the ferry of light reaches the sun, the moon, and the realm above.

∼

SONGS OF THOMAS

Song 9: The Lion and the Beautiful Daughter

The lion took my beautiful daughter. He seized her,
dragged her into his lair with his great dragon.

When she was in the pit, the lion screamed.
His companions gathered. The dragon whistled

and hissed. All the beasts gathered near him
and roared. They hid from my daughter,

roaring elsewhere, lest their powers diminish.
So my cry calls up to the mighty one,

who excels among the powers. I the son ask
my father. My garment hangs

on the universe, saying, If I have wronged
the great lion, let him eat me now in his lair.

If I've wronged the great dragon, let him swallow
me here. But if I haven't wronged the lion

here in his midst, let me escape his lair and take
my daughter from him. Father of us all

place the garment over us all. I pounded
their nets. I cracked open their lair.

I cast stones on it. I seized the great dragon, and his
consort I enmeshed in a trap. I took my daughter

from them and placed her high above them all.
I hurled stones at their wheel till it collapsed

under them, and my daughter and I destroyed
all their nets. We drove the great lion

and the dragon out of the cosmos, and we came
to the village land of the just. They know

it too. From the heart of a second lair I
took my daughter into the land. They now

are also happy. And it will happen soon
just as the bride enters the bridal chamber.

Song 12: Jesus Dug a River

Jesus dug a river in the cosmos. He dug a river,
even he of the sweet name. He dug it with a spade

of truth. He dredged it with a basket of wisdom.
The stones he dredged from it are drops

of incense from Lebanon. All the waters in it
are roots of light. Three ships sail.

They voyage in the river, testing. One is full,
one half freighted. The third is empty.

The full ship sails fearlessly. One half full.
The empty one comes empty

and leaves nothing behind. It will suffer
at the customs. It has nothing to give,

nothing on board. They will tear it apart
wickedly and send it back to the port.

The ship will suffer what corpses suffer. Empty.
They called it and it heard nothing.

Song 20: Cry of Pamoun the Ox

Hear an ox. The cry of Pamoun, an ox. Mercy.
I make the worlds weep.

What have the children of the earth given me?
They grabbed two-edged axes

and stuck me in marshes. They felled fat trees
and even thin ones.

They didn't leave alone. With the fat tree
they cut out a plow.

From the thin one they made a sharp goad.
Then took it to an artist

who in his own hand fashioned a yoke,
stuck it on my neck,

and hooked the plow hanging behind me.
They used the goad

to pierce my ribs. Then they carried me
to the butcher's son,

the fattener of oxen; it was the butcher's
son who chopped me up,

scattered me to foreign tents, hung me
in far markets, and

before anybody tossed my bones to stray
beasts.[2] Release me

from the owners. They don't buy me. They burn
what is inside me,

even that. Don't beat Pamoun, the ox.
Shake the spirit vessels in you.[3]

SONG OF HERAKLEIDES

Come Together

Come together, O sons of the earth, and hear
the angel who was sent out

with the message of the skies.
You came and were a gathering, you came

and they gathered in you.
Tell us the message of the skies.

You came and the aeons were in rank,
you came and they gathered in you.

Tell us
the message of the skies.

Wake, you who sleep.
Wake, you who sleep. Sleep in the cavern

that you can receive the sky's message.
The carrier of the message is on his way

with the message from the land of light
to speak out the message of the skies.

He was sent out. He raced laughing
to the first man to tell him the message.

He came and knocked on the gates
and shouted, Open up at once.

I have the message of the skies!

The Call Is Heard

The call, the call, is once again heard.
I came and they were gathered.

I came and the gods were happy.
I came and they were gathered round me.

Look, this is the message!
I came and the father was gathered.

The aeons were gathered round the father.
Look, this is the message!

Look, this is the message!
The harpists were gathered and the pipes were sonorous.

I was sent out, and the air was ecstatic
to be all gathered and round the father.

I was sent out, and the walls were dug in the earth,
and the sentinels of the towers

were guarding them.
Look, this is the message!

I was sent out, and the father
was sleeping in his quarters in the land of light.

Look, this is the message! I was sent out, and the father
was happy and the virgins encircled him.

Look, this is the message!
I was sent out, and the pipes were sonorous

on the mooring places.
Look, this is the message! I was sent out,

and the sea was placid,
and the raft of heaven was towed out.

Look, this is the message!
I was sent out, and ships touched land,

and the seaports were secured.
Look, this is the message! I came, and the walls

were set in foundations,
and the sentinels on the tower guarded them.

Look, this is the message!

SONG TO JESUS, 264

Ferry Me to the Sun

Take me, firstborn. The path of light
spreads before me from my own first city.

I look for someone. The dissolving image
of the savior comes to me. O first one, the light

of the virgin touches me, the brightest
picture of truth with her three angels

who give grace. Firstborn, the portals of
the sky fly open before me in the rays

of my savior and his portrait of light.
I left my garment on the earth.

Senile diseases were mine. I dress in the deathless
robe. Ferry me to the sun and the moon.

Ferry of light at peace over three earths.
Firstborn, I am a holy bride in her chamber

of light, resting. I keep my victory gift. I have worked;
it is good. My end is happy eternal possession.

O firstborn, glory and conquest for lord Mani,
his holy elect, and for blessed Mary's soul.

WANDERER SONG

O Soul, Sleeping

O soul, sleeping. You who sleep, you who
doze, wake. Sun rises on you. ·

Morning is the truth of the commandments
the dead, the corpses have risen.

Here is the habitat of robbers,
the house of cares and sadnesses.

They are merciless scavengers,
hearing no call. They have no heart

for the condemned. They flatter you
the tree. The good man has come.

Jewel garland, you. Wandering sheep,
your shepherd seeks you. Noble and despised,

your king wants you. Where are
your angelic cloths, robes that don't age?

18

THE GREAT SONG TO MANI

The Great Song to Mani[1] is a late piece of Manichaean poetry. In this song, which incorporates Buddhist terminology, Mani is understood to be Buddha Mani, and he is praised for preaching the true law and rescuing those who suffer. Mani, it is claimed, helps people overcome *samsara,* the wheel of birth and rebirth, and find the bliss of nirvana, and Mani himself attains buddhahood.

You Rescued from Samsara

> We who are miserable and with no hope
> would have stayed in the torture of samsara,[2]
> not finding the end of your path.
> You set up the ladder of wisdom,
> you let us supersede the five forms of being,[3]
> and you delivered us.
>
> We who were fettered in suffering
> were rescued from rebirth

to see the Buddha-like sun god
who is like you.
For those tied to transitory pleasure,
you preached the true law.
You carried them across the sea of suffering
to the good nirvana.[4]
For those tied to the root of attachment to the world,
you revealed the road to the realm of the Buddhas,
you raised a Sumeru mountain of virtue,[5]
you let them find endless happiness.
For those plunged in the water of pride,
you showed the bridge of the true law.
You took understanding of the good law into their hearts.
You entrusted them to the holy assembly.
For those confused by the six organs of perception[6]
you showed the rising and falling states of being.
You revealed what is the suffering of those in the Avici,
the deepest Buddhist hell.
You let them be reborn in the blessed fivefold heaven of light.[7]
Look for the ways of salvation,
you crossed lands going to every side.
When you found humans needing salvation,
you rescued all.

You Preached the Jewel of the Gospel

To those like us who were lazy,
you preached details of the jewel of the gospel book.[8]
We come on the ways of freedom and salvation
when we know them in the book.
If you hadn't preached the pure law so fully,
wouldn't the world and its thinking beings

have come to an end by now?
After the four Buddhas[9] you went down
and attained truly incomparable buddhahood.
You saved thousands
and saved them from dark hell.
You purged them of masterly cunning and deception
and caused them to help others.
You were a guide leading those in error.
You saved them from the claws of evil Mara.[10]
You rescued the malevolent,
you healed the blind,
you caused them to do works of honor,
you showed them the right path to the land of the gods,
You were born the hope and refuge of the world.
You taught the seven precious books[11]
and held back those about to join evil.

19

THE MOTHER
OF BOOKS

The Mother of Books, the Umm al-Kitab,[1] is a book of epic poetry representative of the spirituality of the *ghulat*, the so-called "exaggerators" within early Shi'ite Islam. These religious adherents practiced a form of religion that could be described as messianic, mystical, even gnostic or Manichaean. This selection from the Mother of Books includes part of the major section of the text, in which a revelation about the origin and meaning of the world is given, in dialogue form, from Baqir, as teacher, to Jabir, as the recipient of revelation. Presented with mythic color, apocalyptic fire, and mystical power, the revelation describes the glories, angels, and colors of the cosmic realm, along with the god who remains exalted above it all. The imagery employed within the text is reminiscent of the opening chapters of Genesis and gnostic interpretations of Genesis, and the text demonstrates its points with reference to proof texts from the Qur'an. The Mother of Books highlights moments in the life of Muhammad the prophet, his family members, and those around, in order to proclaim creation, the fall into disbelief, and the return to knowledge and salvation.

Among the characters and terms in the text, Ali, Fatima, Hasan, and Husayn are members of the family of Muhammad; Boraq is the winged horse, and Duldul the white mule of Muhammad; Salman is a follower of Ali and here the spiritual regent of god, with similarities to personified wisdom and the heavenly human in gnostic texts; Iblis is the devil; and Azazi'il is an arrogant angel who resembles the arrogant creator of this world in gnostic texts.

~

The Essential Mystery

Jabir rose to his feet, saying, "My lord,
tell me the meaning of the holy phrase,
Bismillah al-rahman al-rahim.
These words meaning 'In the name of Allah,
the compassionate, the merciful' begin
each chapter of the Qur'an. And many
recite them before doing anything.
All know them as the essential mystery."

Baqir said, "They are from the high king, who is god.
He wrote them as the loftiest line on earth:
seven and twelve parts the king made for himself.
Overhead he made a sea of a thousand colors
and below another sea named godliness.
Between the seas the king placed seven and twelve deathless
uncreated lights, his ears and eyes. As written in the Qur'an,
'He let two great bodies of water flow. They meet
with a barrier to halt their commingling.'

"Jabir, the large bodies of water are two seas,
the barrier is the king, their pearls and coral
are the Naqib and Najib angels. They are dazzling
lights and lamps joining realms to believers' hearts.
By the highest god, here is knowledge flowing
from paradise to paradise and hell to hell,
and nothing has been written of these events.

The Seven and Twelve Light Our Form and Body

"Jabir, the seven and twelve also light our form
and body. So the brain is the white sea,
and the spirit of speech is the high king
found in the medulla. Two eyes, two ears,
two nostrils, and the mouth are seven parts
of the high king. Two hands with ten fingers
are the twelve parts dividing the white sea
and remote eternal sphere. And in that sphere
is the high king's canopy over our heads.

"The sphere is the great spirit of a thousand colors.
The brain is the white earth over seven skies
as the white sea lies over seven realms
of a heavenly palace. As it is written, 'A revelation
from him who created the earth and heaven.
The merciful one sat on the throne possessing
all in the skies, on earth, and in between
and underground.' God is on the white sea
as the high king's throne—he is all powerful!

Our Features Also Reflect Bismillah's Letters

"Our human features were created to prove
this mystery. The right ear, eye, nostril,
and language reflect *ba* and *sin* and *mim*,
and language is the dot under the *ba*.[2]
The left ear, eye, and nostril become *lams*
and *mim* and *ha*. The holy spirit of life
on the forehead is the sign and proof
of *alif* in the middle, and these parts

figured on our head are the spirit's tools.
The ears are set at both sides for eternity.
Quicker than a wink they inform life spirit."

What Is the Creator of This World Like?

Jabir rose to his feet, wiped his face with his hand,
and asked, "My lord, is the creator in heaven
or on earth? What is he and where is he from?
What does he look like? What virtues has he?
Where is he from and what has he created?"

The revealer of knowledge—may our salvation
come from him—said, "Jabir, these are hard questions.
Forget them. It's wrong to open the curtain
before the high king. It is a grave sin.
No prophet or spirit has ever drawn open
the curtain, even a slit, to reveal the king.
No book has ever recorded his face.
Keep this book for yourself and the believers.

The Five Preexistent Lights

"Before the sky or earth or any creature,
there were five preexistent lights in five colors
like the rainbow. Sublime air issued like sun
from sparks of light and spread over the sky
and earth. The five lights stood in this air,
and a glow came out of the belly of light
continuously and in five colors: hearing,
sight, smell, taste, and speech. The five lights
are Muhammad, Ali, Fatima, Hasan,

and Husayn. They came from nothing. As it is written,
'Speak out that he is god, one sovereign god.
He did not father children, nor was he fathered;
there's none like him.' Around believers' heads
these five lights swim around the throne of god.

The Spirit of Speech Sits in the Sea on the Brain

"The spirit of speech sits among them. He is the god
of truth. He creates and appears in each name
and body, from the loftiest of summits
down to the profoundest depths. Jabir,
I said, the lord is spirit through his godliness
and sun through light. Through spirituality
he has been called the spirit of speech. He sits
in the white sea on the brain of the believers.
His is color of lightning, clouds, and moon.

God's Form and Attributes

"Here is god's form. His right hand is retention
that comprehends and is the color of sun.
His left hand is the spirit of thought. From it
comes the full propagation of all light.
'No. Spreading his hands, he gives as he wishes,'
and this spirit is the color violet.
God's head is the grandest spirit composed
of all kinds of colors, a thousand of them.
There is nothing higher than he, neither
in heaven nor on earth. 'There is nothing
that might be his equal. He hears and sees.'

"His right eye is a huge spirit, the color
of white crystal. His left eye is the spirit
of the intellect, color of red yellow fire.

"His two ears are an intense mixing of
the rays of color from the holy veil.

"The lord's nostrils are the spirit of knowledge,
one the color of red carnelian, exuding everywhere
a floating holy perfume. The other nostril
is the spirit of the almighty, green
from god's breath and radiance. His tongue
is the voice of holy spirit, the color of red rubies.

"The heart of the lord is the spirit of faith,
whose name is the confessor of one true faith
and who is the color of the sphere of the moon.

"On the day of resurrection the lord
will place his foot across hell and freeze it.

"The lord's throne is this godly seat, the brain.
The right half of the brain is the spirit
of wisdom, and the left is the spirit of abundance.
The lord sits in his majesty. As it is written,
'The merciful set himself on the throne.'
These five lights, visible from eight angles,
are reflected on the believers' faces
and compose the lord's throne: of two eyes, ears,
nostrils, speech, and spirit perceiving taste."

The Order of the Heavenly Realms

Jabir said, "My lord, if you will, enlighten me.
Tell your servant the face, sense, and majesty
of holy realms, of light joining realm to realm."

Baqir said, "First comes the curtain of eternity
on the white sea and the form of the high king.
Muhammad, Ali, Fatima, Hasan, and Husayn
are of this realm, finished by Abu Talib
and Abdallah. These five angels' five lights
join the white sea like trees of paradise.

"Five creatures sit in five trees in the first, white sphere:
The lion, Boraq, the white falcon, the royal phoenix,
and Duldul, who is the sign of godliness,
sit on the top of five trees, singing praise,
happiness, honor, and glory from the leaves:
'All on heaven and earth glorify god,
most holy king, the powerful and wise.'
Boraq comes from the light of Muhammad,
Duldul from the light of Ali, the lion
from the light of Fatima, the white falcon
from the light of Hasan, the royal phoenix
comes from the glittering light of Husayn.

"The white sea is decorated with them.
In all this vastness in the white sphere,
a thousand times greater than other realms,
lies 'a garden as great as sky and earth.'

The Ruby Red Curtain

"Below this white dome is a curtain red
like a ruby. In this curtain five creatures
appear in five Tuba trees. The ruby curtain
is believable down to the last sphere.
In rainbow colors 124,000 lights
on the white sea glitter to the last sphere
where 124,000 white lights
came to the ruby curtain. As it is written,
'Have you not seen that god created seven layers
of skies and how he placed the moon as light
and sun as lamp? God made you grow in earth
like plants.' The high one fastened many lights
and spirits to these spheres, and then he placed
the sun and moon and glowing trees as beauty."

The Beginning of Creation Springs from Azazi'il

Then Jabir stood, prayed, and said, "My Lord,
how did the high king create all these spheres
and palaces? From where did he make the spirits?
What was the origin of his creation?"

The revealer of knowledge—may we be blessed—
said, "The creation of these realms is hard
to fathom. Not everyone knows the way
to knowledge, and its secret's well concealed.
Jabir, in the beginning there was god,
only eternal god and nothing else,
but in the middle of five special lights

the high king shone, as told in the beginning
of this book. All the heavens and the earth
were nothing but pure clear fine spiritual air.
From five specific elements came five
lights of the farthest realms, and they contained
some 124,000 hues,
and every moment was another color.

"Those special elements were members of
the farthest dome. A hundred thousand shining
lights, candles, and lamps emerged from the depths
of the high king in that dome, moving from
nonbeing to being. As it is written, 'Questions of
the hour are but a second.' No one knows
the majesty of angels, of angelic beings
and creatures. If the seas turned into ink
and trees were writing instruments, the seven
heavens were paper, and the spirits and beings
of lights, jinns, and humans began to write
and wrote about the appearance and majesty
of the eternal farthest dome, all would be used,
less than a thousandth of it written down,
fulfilling words of god, 'Look, if the sea
were ink for words of my lord, it would
dry up before seizing words of my lord.'

"Then the high king's cries echoed left and right.
The two cries then converted into beams,
and these two beams were pure uncounted spirits.
Each spirit was made of seven colors, each
color a million colors like the rubies
from Badahsan, carnelian, coral,
turquoise, emerald, and pearls. And each joint beamed

its light like a clear star, and as our fingers
and toes have nails, so every moon or sun
shone from each nail. They were in six circles,
and each group had a leader and an elder.
The master was Azazi'il, and his
six ranks of elders went from one to six.

In His Image and Arrogance Azazi'il Creates from Light

"The high king lent Azazi'il light, and using
this light he shaped his creations.
In his image he made spirits. The king
shouted about what he had done. Azazi'il shouted
his creation of place, aeon, and spirit into being,
and no one but the high king knows how many.[3]

"The high king said to Azazi'il, 'Old man,
tell me who you are and what I am
and what all these creatures are.' Azazi'il
answered, 'You are a god and I'm a god,
and all these spirits both of us have made.'[4]

"The high king said, 'There cannot be two gods.
You're my creation. I'm the one who's made
these spirits,' in fulfillment of god's word;
'I will create a person out of clay.'

"Azazi'il said, 'What I've made is more
than yours; yes, I've made ten times more than you.
How can you dare claim your divinity?'

The High King Takes Back the Light from Azazi'il

"The high king captured Azazi'il's light,
saying, 'These creatures you have made I made
also. If I withdraw the gift I loaned you,
how will you create?' He took from Azazi'il
the light he'd loaned him and the creatures
that had been made with it, and from it
he made a dome of a white sea a thousand times
larger than the blue dome of earthly sky.
He made 124,000 lamps,
flickering candles, and brightly burning lights
appear, and painted palaces and castles
out of white crystal in 100,000 colors,
and he adorned them with the flowing rivers
of the water of life and on the riverbanks
the Tuba tree. In branches of the trees
the royal phoenix sat, and in its shade
were young men and boys. The white falcon, Duldul,
Boraq, and the lion adorned this white sphere.
On branches he created the wood pigeon,
turtledove, and nightingale, beautiful
beyond description. 'Nothing had been made
like him. He is the one who hears and sees.'

"After the high king fashioned the white dome
in all its beauty, he told Azazi'il,
'Make another sea equal to the one
that I have made.' After the king said this,
Azazi'il was shocked. He could not make
such a creation. And as it is written, 'Those
who won't believe are doomed to nothingness.'
'God doesn't lead those lacking faith in him.'

The High King Creates More Glorious Beings

"The high king wanted to create more beings
and showed this, shouting out his echo ahead
and behind, and when it reached the horizons
of the holy realm, everything rebounded
the echo of the two shouts, and from them
arose six tiers of spirits a thousand times
more delicate and pure. They were embellished
with pearls, corals, and rubies. A light shone
from every joint, a sun from every sinew.
A clear moon sparkled out of its navel.

"The high king glorified himself and from him
all learned to glorify and became glorifiers.
The senior in these six ranks was his Salman.[5]
The others said, 'This place is beautiful,
and the form god has given us is beautiful.
If the godhead who created us appeared,
we'd testify he gave us paradise
and beauty's forms would be with us forever.'

"Then the high king turned to them, saying, 'I am
Allahu akbar, I am *Allahu akbar.*'
The spirits were amazed, not knowing whether
the high king spoke for himself or someone else.
When some time passed, the high king said again,
'I am *Allahu akbar,* I am *Allahu akbar,*'
which means, 'I am your great god and creator.'

Azazi'il Rebels and Falls from Glory

"The king said to Azazi'il, 'Azazi'il,
lie on the ground before Salman. All followers
lie on the ground before the foremost who
confirm Salman or I will cast you down
below.' As it is written, 'When we said to the angels,
"Lie down before Adam," they all lay down
except for Iblis, who arrogantly refused.
He was faithless.'

"Then Azazi'il
turned to the king. He was a fool and claimed
divinity.[6] A second and a third
arose and came to aid Azazi'il.
They claimed divinity, calling the king
a common liar and a thief, a trickster,
and then they said that 'god is one of three.'[7]

"The six denying ranks turned on Salman
and battled him at length with arrogance.
The high king said, 'You unbelieving demons,
corruption, rebels! You attempt to rule
this realm and the eternal far white sea,
but you cannot rule unless you will affirm
me and my regent.' This fulfills god's word,
'Jinns and humans! You try to penetrate
the precincts of the sky and of the earth,
but without my permission you will fail!'

The Denying Ranks Are Confined

"Then the high king gave orders to Salman,
'We cannot leave these beings in this state.
From seven lights I made to cloak the faithless,
turn ruby light into a ruby curtain.
Transform the fire light, and make a curtain
from it, and keep them muffled in the cloth
and cover the white eternal farthest sea
with this curtain, color of ruby.' As it is written,
'We told you all to fall from paradise.'

"Right then Salman began to terrorize,
seizing the ruby light, and cloaking them
as by a ruby dome, cloaked the white sea
and farthest dome. He stripped them of their fire,
spreading it out below them. They lived
between these curtains for a thousand years.

Azazi'il Continues His Rebellion

"Azazi'il stayed with six groups of beings
locked in this paradise a thousand years.
After the thousand years the high creator
appeared behind the curtain of Salman
and said clearly, 'I am god.' Azazi'il
denied him and again he was the fool.
This denial is mentioned in the Qur'an,
where it says, 'When we said to the angels,
"Lie down before Adam," they all lay down
except for Iblis. He said, "Should I bow
before one whom you fashioned out of clay?"

He asked, "What kind of king is this? You showered
more honor on him than me. If you'll grant me
a chance to wait until the resurrection,
I'll murder his descendants, save a few."
God said, "Go away. Whoever follows you,
hell will be his reward. Wake whom you can,
use your armies to incite them, take up
their fortune and their children, promise them
all kinds of things. Satan makes lying vows.
But you have no command over my servants.'"

"They fought a horrid and horrific battle
against the high king. Then the high creator
ordered Salman, 'We have no use for them
in paradise. Take the sun-colored light
from them and spread it out below them all.'
Salman struck terror in their ranks. He cut
them off from sun-colored light and turned
it into sun water, spread it below,
adorned it with great tons of light and color,
the sun and moon. Azazi'il was imprisoned
with all his beings. He cloaked his violet realm
with realms of sun. His beings stayed behind
the curtain of the sun a thousand years.

This World Is Made Colorless

"God made the world framed with appalling mountains,
expansive deserts, profound seas, and beasts
and birds from substances of the six ranks
of faithless. Then he took away the color
of the world. Prolonged time passed without day
or darkness, when there was no time or name
or any soul across the dry cracked earth.

The World Comes to Life

"Then the high king flung out denying spirits,
the faithless minds, flung them out of the kingdom
down onto earth, and then he gave the world
a breath, a spirit, and it came to life.
Vegetation and plants sprang from the earth,
and through his force vegetation and plants
were fashioned from the substance of the cursed,
proceeding from the shout of Azazi'il.

"This vegetative spirit spread everywhere
across the earth. And then the high king chose
to regenerate the seven colors taken
from Azazi'il: red, black, blue, violet,
indigo blue, yellow, and white. He called
them clouds and returned water to the streams
and rivers, scattering them over the earth,
keeping the earth moistened and fresh. And steam
in the spirit's world became the angel whom
the high king consigned to the clouds. He fulfilled
his words, 'The thunders praise him, as do angels.'"

This Describes the Body as Microcosm

Jabir said, "My lord, what can be the proof
that the highest command descends from clouds?"

Baqir answered, "Here is truth. Each particle
of holy light sent through this cloud down to
the path of breathing earth is consonant
with the highest command. The cloud itself

consists of substance of Azazi'il.
Jabir, if clouds were not from Azazi'il,
the sun and moon sloping along their spheres
would not be hidden to the waverers.
Azazi'il shows in the microcosm
with seven faces: evil thoughts and greed,
jealousy, doubt, uncertainty. The glow
of faith's spirit and the intelligible sun
are also hidden from the spirit of lust.

"Clouds of the macrocosm are combined
with light of the high king as a nude body
combines with spirit. And the other cloud,
highest in the command, is spirit's speech,
color of cloud, the thunder and lightning
and the moon's rain are knowledge of the light.
The earth on which it tumbles is the heart,
the sky from which it comes is spirit's faith,
its sphere is language: 'All float in a sky.'

The High King Wants to Create People on Earth

"Then the high king said, 'I want to make
people on earth, endowing them dominion
over the world.' 'When the lord told his angels,
I will send a successor to the earth,'
they became three nations. One nation said,
'God does what he wants to.' 'And he decides
his ways. You want it solely at god's desire.'

"Others said, 'Why place someone on this earth
who unjustly sheds blood, who commits acts
of shame?' 'Azazi'il rebelled and others rose

in the madness of his misery, and said,
"If you create someone else in this world,
we will not prostrate ourselves before him.'"

"The high king said, 'Come before waverers
and bow down before everything above you,
and before those who know the earth and heavens
and those who know the plants and growing things.'
The angels could not comprehend, but waverers
explained the knowledge of the earth and heavens,
the names of plants and growing things, mountains
and all on earth. 'He taught Adam the names
and then he showed them to the angels.'

Iblis, Who Is Satan, Rebels; Shadows and Phantoms Appear

"Iblis and his people who had the form of fire
rebelled and showed their disbelief. 'We won't
bow down before them, we're better than they.'
'You fashioned me of fire but him of clay.'
The high king grew furious. He said to them,
'The covering will fall off all of you—
and this is hell—and you will wander proud
no longer, but you'll linger in those tight
and black and body-hugging darkest forms.'

Humans Are Evicted from Paradise

"When the high king came in, he howled against
the lingerers, 'Get out of here, all of you.
Get out of paradise. Assume the form
of thin dark shadows.' He hurled them away
into their shadowy shape, and had women
appear with deep vaginas and with breasts."

How the Individual Comes to Knowledge and Is Saved

Then Jabir said, "My lord, when will the spirit
and heart be saved?"[8]
Baqir answered, "A spirit
of conviction living in the heart is witness
to divinity and leaves the heart and goes
into the brain, if it has witnessed clearly.
And even after worship from the highest
heaven and from the earth, it won't accept
anything but witnessing described as just
in Muhammad's Qur'an, a testimony
for current imams, whose appearance is
the paradise of the exalted king.

"Their speech provides the gate to paradise,
the place of Salman, and the site where orphans
bow and where seven angels say their prayers,
the realm of the Naqib, the palace of the Najib,
the dome of Adam and the ark of Noah,
the priestly robes of Abraham, the tablets
of Moses, the summit of Jesus, and the throne
where Muhammad the chosen lives, along
with the thirty-legged footstool of Ali,
the prince of the believers, and the garden
of Fatima, and paradise of Hasan and Husayn,
the bridge of the believers. They make up
the refuge of the cherubim, the spheres
of beings of light, direction of the prayer
of spiritual beings. The high king said,
I do not wish you to turn east and west
to say your prayer. The eternal god prefers
you turn to the good imams and believe

in their prophetic light, in every show
of light, and every palace, realm, aeon,
and cycle, each location of the deity,
the kingdom, the great lord, the glory and
eternity of godliness, the light,
spirit, humanity, the flesh, and imam.

"Everywhere you must testify to him
and sacrifice possessions, blood, and power
to build a dam to hold back death and need,
hunger and poverty, grave sicknesses
and all the world's catastrophes. What happens
to you in any form, be patient; suffer it.
In all things fear judgment, try to grow nearer to god,
and be on guard against this awful world.
Have faith. And thus you fulfill god's word,
'Goodness does not require you to turn
your face to east or west. It asks you to believe
in god and the last day, the angels, scripture,
and prophets.' The last day is a great day.
Believe in these words and believe in light
of the high king's regent, Salman, who is
the word of god. For everything in heaven
and on the earth is also in the word of god,
and nothing on dry land or in the sea
is not part of his word, 'and there is nothing,
wet or dry, not recorded in his word.'"

Where Does This Secret Knowledge Come From?

Then Jabir said, "My lord, is the final testimony
from us or from the will and glory
of the high king? When the inspired who know
sit on the carpet of the great lord, the curtain

of light is raised and your students testify.
Where does this secret knowledge come from?"

Baqir answered, "Get away from bad students
as from the avarice of those who know."

Jabir said, "My lord, explain to your low servant."

Baqir said, "Be careful. These words are difficult.
By Muhammad and the glorified, by Ali
the highest, these are words not written in
a book. One keeps them secret. Jabir, if
the right imam and the inspired who knows
reveals the truth to students, the pupil
would not accept it and the heart's spirit
could not absorb it. The speaking spirit
of life is all alone. Then at the bidding
of the high king, with the purpose and will
of the imam, a spirit of lightning color
will come down from the blue dome and enter
the student's brain and spirit of the heart.
The spirit of the heart believes in glory
and words of one who knows and testifies
in truth of the convinced. At the will of the
high king, the shining spirit descends from
the moon-colored curtain and searches out
the tested spirit, speaker for the teacher.
The spirit of the heart of students hears
this word and testifies to godliness
of one who knows, but his rank is incapable
of holding the word in his memory.

"Then by the will of one who knows, the spirit
of retention descends from the sun-colored
curtain, and it enters faith's spirit.

The word remains in memory, but he
has not the strength to think of it. But sent
by the high king, thought's spirit comes down from
the violet-colored curtain and resides
in his retention. The spirit of the heart
thinks of this thought and understands the words
of one who knows but who lacks strength to speak
before the one who truly knows the word.

"Then the almighty's spirit descends from
the emerald green curtain and enters thought.
The student's heart floats overhead and in
his limbs he clearly sees the holy realm.
These words are clear but are not from the curtain
until the will of one who knows the light
of spirit and of wisdom descends from
the agate-colored realm and joins the spirit
of the high lord. This spirit is gifted with language,
and light of knowledge speaks before the one
who knows. It is not perfect yet, and one
who knows has not approved it. Then intellect
comes down from the realm, the color of fire,
and enters knowledge. Finally the student
understands clearly and hears the words
of one who knows. He cannot yet transcend
his sensual soul, the spirit of desire, and the rebuked Adam,
until the holy spirit appears from the dome
of red ruby and enters his spirit.

"The spirit of the student's heart crushes
the three souls tempting sin in him, kills them,
and as the seven components, heart, head, lungs, liver,
spleen, bladder   he destroys the seven
unbelievers who have lived in his soul,

and Iblis's cycle is over now.
The lusting in his penis and testicles
is dead, the spirit of the heart awakes
at night and fasts by day. A human still is
not about to rise to heaven. He'll get there
if by the will of the high king and through
the light of one who knows and the resolution
of the disciple a great universal spirit
descends from the white dome and enters in
the student's holy spirit. Then spirit of
the student's heart will climb a few steps higher
from the house of wind and hover in
the commanding arteries of his chest.

"Body and matter will be bright and light
because of light of godliness and holy
revelation. God says, 'Is there anyone
whose chest god has expanded for Islam
so he's enlightened by the lord?' But spirit
of the heart still can't reach the brain. Great spirit
descends from under the high king's canopy,
in the remotest realm, at the command
and by the will of the high king and with
the purpose of good imams, landing perfectly
on the great universal spirit. Then
the spirit of the heart can move from chest
to lips, tongue, and mouth, and end up on
the holy throne. The one who knows arises
and testifies to spirit as to himself.

"The student will be perfect, and ten spirits
are spoken for. God says, 'These are the perfect ten.'
The ten stanzas of the Qur'an also
convey the ten Islamic ranks, ten days

of feast,[9] the counting going up to ten
and when it gets to ten begins again,
and every number ten around the world
stands for it too. That's why we call this book
the ten speeches, and this description resides
uniquely in this book and in no other."

20

THE GOSPEL OF
THE SECRET SUPPER

The Gospel of the Secret Supper, or John's Interrogation,[1] is a text that bears witness to the flowering of gnosis in gnostic or Neomanichaean form among the Bogomils and Cathars in western Europe during medieval times and in the years after. Originally obtained from the Bogomils, the Secret Supper is a dualistic gospel that features the invisible father, his son the angel Christ, and John of the canonical gospels, who questions the lord (Christ) and the invisible father at a last supper. In the dialogue that ensues (here somewhat shortened), Christ tells the story of Satan and his interactions with the world and people in the world—Satan's fall, his activity in creation, his role as prince of this world, and his ultimate demise. At the end of time, it is declared, Satan will be bound and detained in a lake of fire, but the elect will shine like the sun in the realm of the invisible father.

~

Who Brought You Here?

I, John, who am your brother and share with you the tribulation of having shared the kingdom of the skies, since I was lying on the chest of our lord Jesus Christ, asked him, "Lord, who brought you here?"

And he answered me, "He who put his hand in the plate with me. So Satan entered in him, and he, Judas, had already betrayed me."

Before Satan Fell

And I said, "Lord, before Satan fell, what was his glory beside your father's?"

And he told me, "Such was his glory that he governed the virtues of heaven. As for me, I sat next to my father. Satan was the master of all those who imitated the father, and his power descended from the sky to the inferno and rose again from the inferno to the throne of the invisible father. And he observed the glory of him who transformed the skies. And he dreamed of placing his seat on the clouds of heaven, because he wanted to be like the very high.

Then, having descended into the air, he said to the angel of the air, "Open the gates of the air for me."

And the angel opened the gates of the air.

And he went on his way to the bottom. There he found the angel who guarded the waters, and he said to him, "Open the gates of the waters for me."

And the angel opened the gates of the waters.

Going ahead, he found the whole face of the earth and saw two fish who were stretched over the waters. They were like two oxen joined together for plowing and, at the invisible father's order, they held up the earth, from sunset to sunrise.

When he descended farther down, he found himself in the presence of clouds weighing on the tidal waves of the sea. He went on until he got to his *ossop,* which is the principle of fire.[2] After that he could not descend farther because of the intense flame of the fire. Then Satan came in from behind and filled his own heart with malice, and reaching the angel of the air and the one who was above the waters, he said to them, "Everything belongs to me. If you listen to me, I will place my seat on the clouds and I shall be similar to the very high. I will withdraw the waters of the upper firmament and assemble all the areas occupied by the sea into one entity of vast seas. That done, there will be no water on the face of the entire earth, and I shall reign with you through the centuries of the centuries."

After he said this, the angel Satan rose toward the other angels to the fifth heaven, and to each of them he said, "How much do you owe your masters?"

"One hundred measures of wheat," one of them answered.

"Take pen and ink," he said to him, "and write forty."

He told the others, "And you, how much do you owe the lord?"

"One hundred jars of oil," he answered him.

"Sit down," Satan said to him, "and write fifty."

He climbed into the skies, and with such words seduced the angels of the invisible father up to the fifth heaven.

The Father Pities Satan

But a voice came out of the throne of the father, saying, "What are you doing, denier of the father, you who are seducing the angels? Creator of sin, hurry with what you hope to do!"

Then the father ordered his angels, "Rip off their robes!"

The angels stripped all those angels who had listened to Satan of their robes, their thrones, and their crowns. And I questioned the lord further.

"When Satan plummeted, where did he make his living place?"

And he responded to me, "My father transformed him because of his pride, and he withdrew the light from him. His face became like red fire and was fully like that of a man. He dragged with his tail the third part of the angels of god, and he was hurled from his seat and from his domain in the skies. Descending to the firmament of the fallen angels, he found no place to rest for himself or for those who were with him.

And he begged the father, saying, "Be patient with me and I will return everything to you!"

The father pitied him and gave him and those with him rest and permission to do what he wished to do on the seventh day.

Satan Reveals Dry Land and Creates Man and Woman

So he installed himself in his heaven and commanded his angels who were above the air and above the waters. He lifted two parts of the water, from bottom to top, into the air, and from the third part he made the sea, which became the mistress of the waters, but, according to the father's commandment, he also prescribed that the angel who was above the waters hold up the two fish. And he lifted the earth from bottom to top and dry land appeared. He took the crown of the angel who commanded the waters and from one half made the light of the moon, from the other the light of the stars. With precious stones he made the army of stars. Then he chose the angels for his ministers according to the celestial hierarchies established by the very high. And by command of the invisible father, he made thunder, the rains, the frosts, and the snows. He placed his angels as ministers over them to govern them. And he commanded the earth to produce every kind of great beast, all reptiles, and trees and grasses. And he commanded the sea to produce fish and the sky birds.

After that he reflected, and he made a man so that he might have a slave. He ordered the angel of the third sky to enter this body of mud, from which he then took out a part for making another body in the form of a woman. And he commanded the angel of the second sky to enter the body of the woman. But these angels wept when they saw that they had there an external mortal form and that they were dissimilar in that external form.[3] Satan joined them in this act of turning their bodies of mud into flesh. The angels did not perceive that in this way he also committed a sin.

The announcer of coming evils meditated in his spirit on a way he would fashion paradise. Then he ordered the people to enter it and his angels to lead them to it. The devil planted a reed in the middle of paradise. And in one spit he made the serpent, whom he commanded to live in the reed. In such way the devil concealed his evil design so they might not know his trickery.

And he entered paradise and spoke with them.

He said to them, "Eat from all the fruit that is found in paradise, but beware of eating the fruit of the knowledge of good and evil."

However, the devil slipped into the body of the evil serpent and seduced the angel who was in the form of woman and he spread over her head the powerful desire of sin, and he satiated Eve with his bodily desire while he attended to the serpent's tail.[4] That is why humans are called the children of the devil and children of the serpent, because they serve the desire of the devil, who is their father, and will serve it until the consummation of this century.

Adam and Eve Choose Sin and Become Mortal

Then, I, John, questioned the lord, "How can one say that Adam and Eve were created by god and placed in paradise to obey the father's orders, but they were then delivered to death?"

The lord answered me, "Listen, John, beloved of my father, it is the ignorant who say, in their error, that my father made these bodies of mud. In reality he created all the virtues of heaven through the holy spirit. But it is through their sin that they found themselves with mortal bodies of mud and were consequently turned over to death."

And again I, John, questioned the lord, "How can a man become born in spirit in a body of flesh?"

And the lord answered, "Descended from angels fallen from the sky, men enter the body of a woman and receive the desire of the flesh. Spirit is born then from the spirit and flesh from the flesh. So Satan accomplishes his reign in this world and in all nations."

He told me further, "My father permitted him to rule seven days, which are seven centuries."

Satan's Angel Chooses Three Trees for the Crucifixion

And again I asked the lord. I said to him, "What did he do during all that time?"

And he told me, "From the instant the devil was expelled from the glory of the father and was forbidden to take part in affairs of heaven, he sat on the clouds and sent his ministers, angels burning with fire, down below to the people. He did so from the time of Adam to Enoch. And he raised his minister Enoch above the firmament and revealed his divinity to him. He had pen and ink brought to him. And once seated, Enoch wrote sixty-seven books under the devil's dictation, and the devil ordered him to carry them back to earth.

Enoch kept them safely on the earth and then transmitted them to his children, and he began to teach them the way to celebrate sacrifices and iniquitous mysteries. So he concealed from people the kingdom of the skies.

And Satan said to them, "See that I am your god and that there is no other god but me." That is why my father sent me into the world, that I make known and teach people to perceive the wicked spirit of the devil. But then Satan, having learned that I had descended from the sky to this world, sent his angel, and he took the wood of three trees and gave it to Moses so that I might be crucified on a cross made from the wood, which is at this time waiting for me. And he made his divinity known to his people, and ordered the law to be given to the children of Israel, and that he cross dry through the middle of the Red Sea.

The Lord Inseminates the Angel Mary

When my father thought of sending me to the earth, he sent before me his angel named Mary to receive me. Then I came down, entered her by the ear, and came out of her ear.[5]

And Satan, prince of this world, knew that I had come down to seek and save the beings who had perished, and he sent his angel the prophet Elijah down to earth to baptize in water. He is called John the baptizer. Then Elijah asked the prince of this world, "How can I recognize the Christ?"

And the lord himself answered, saying, "He on whom you will see the holy spirit descend like a dove and remain there, he is immersed in the holy spirit for the remission of his sins. He alone has the power to lead astray and to save."

Heaven or the Lake of Fire

And then I asked the lord about the day of judgment, "What will be the sign of your coming?"

He answered me, "It will be when the name of the just will be consummated according to the name of the just ones who have been crowned and fallen from the sky. Then Satan will be freed and will leave his prison, a prey to great anger, and he will make war on the just and they will cry to the lord god in a great voice. And the lord will immediately command his angel to sound the trumpet. The voice of the archangel, in the trumpet, will be heard from heaven to the inferno. And then the sun will darken and the moon give no more light. The stars will fall and the four winds will be torn from the foundations, and they will make the earth tremble, and also the mountains and hills. Immediately the sky will tremble and the sun darken until the fourth hour. Then will appear the earthly son, and with him all the saintly angels. And then the son rises, and he will place his seat on the clouds and will sit on the throne of his majesty, with twelve messengers seated on twelve chairs of glory.

He will say to the sinners, "Go far from me, cursed ones, into the eternal fire that has been prepared for the devil and for his angels."

Then all the others, seeing that the time has come for the ultimate separation, will pity the sinners in their inferno, who will be there by order of the invisible father.

The souls will leave the prison of the unbelievers and also my voice will be heard, and there will be no more than one sheepfold and one pastor. And there will issue from the depths of the earth a dark gloom, which is the dark gloom of the Gehenna of fire, and fire will consume the universe from the abysses of the earth to the air of the firmament. And the lord will reign from the firmament to the infernos of the earth. The lake of fire where the sinners will live is so deep that a stone that a thirty-year-old man lifts and drops to the bottom will barely reach the floor of the lake after three years.

Satan in Fire and the Elect in Heaven

Then Satan will be bound with all his troops and placed in the lake of fire. But the son of god and his elect will stroll on the firmament, and he will lock the devil, lying there, in strong, indestructible chains. The sinners weeping and lamenting will say, "Earth, take us back and hide us in you."

The just will glow like a sun in the kingdom of the invisible father. And the son of god will take them before the throne of the invisible father and say to them, "Here I am with my children whom you have given me. Just father, the world has not known you, but I have truly known you, because it is you who sent me on my mission."

Then the son of god will sit at the right of the father, and the father will govern his angels and govern the elect. He will place them in choirs of angels, dress them in imperishable garments, and give them unfading crowns and immutable seats. And god will be seated in the middle of them. They will not know hunger or thirst. The sun will not strike them, nor any burning heat. And god will banish all tears from their eyes. The son will reign with his saintly father, and his reign will have no end from centuries to centuries.

21

A NUN'S SERMON

The final text in this book is the Nun's Sermon, or more properly "A Nun's Sermon to Ladies Carenza, Iselda, and Alais on Priority of Knowledge and Light over Earthly Body."[1] This text, added here as a conclusion to this collection of sacred texts of knowledge and wisdom, is a Cathar poem, given in a woman's voice, supposedly by a nun, on the satisfaction and thrill of marrying god—who is, after all, the crown of knowledge and light.

~

My lady Carenza of the lovely body,
please offer sisters your profound advice,
and since you know what's best, tell us
precisely what to do. You know. Your ways embody
all ways of woman. Please say: shall I wed
someone we know? Or stay a virgin? I've said
that would be good. But having kids—what for?
To me a marriage seems a painful bore.

Lady Carenza, I'd like to have a man,
but what a penance when you have a clan
of brats. Your tits hang halfway to the ground;
your belly is discomfited and round.

My lady Iselda and my lady Alais,
you have youth, beauty; your skin a fresh color
and you know courtly manners; you have valor
beyond all other women in your place.

Hear me. And for the best seed from a cod,
marry the crown of knowledge, who is GOD.
And you will bear the fruit in glorious sons,
saving your chastity like married nuns.

My lady Iselda and my lady Alais,
remember me and may my light transcend
all fears. Please ask the king of glory,
when you enter heaven, to join us once again.

EPILOGUE

The Inner Light of Gnosis:
A Historical Meditation

WILLIS BARNSTONE

The specific origin of gnosticism is unknown—and may be unknowable. It is unknown not because gnosticism sprang from nowhere and nothing. Indeed, we know approximately when and where this dualistic movement of a god of light spirit and a god of dark matter began in antiquity, and also the names of the possible sources. But there are deeply conflicting theses, ancient and modern, about the relevance of these sources to the origin of the widespread and enduring global sect. The story of the origin of most of the world's spiritual movements—Daoism, Hinduism, Buddhism, Zoroastrianism, and Judaism—is blurred in possibility, and reaches us more as legend than history. Even highly documented early Christianity, born of two essential Jewish scriptures, the Old and New Testaments, is steeped in the legends of the New Testament gospels, its core source, that disguise rather than reveal historical probability. So the word is still out on gnosticism. It has backers who speak of elements of Jewish, Christian, Zoroastrian, Buddhist, Platonic, Alexandrian Neoplatonic, and Egyptian hermetic ancestry.

Is there one or are there multiple progenitors of gnosticism? While many favor a multiple-source thesis, the diverse appearances of gnostic thought in the Near East and Alexandria have enough commonality to suggest a unifying spirit in the air, transcending sect, language, and geography. Two singular ideas separate the dualistic gnostics from the old Greco-Roman theologies, Judaism, and emerging Christianity: (1) an assumption of two divinities finding their way into us—one of spirit and eternal light, the other of darkness and temporal body; and (2) a transcendent principle of light that may be found during one's lifetime, in a flash of gnosis, bringing divinity into one's solitude.

In gnosticism, salvation, as the flash of gnosis, may be achieved now and not only as a reward after death, as in Christianity. Christian salvation—unseeable, untestifiable, unexperienced by humans—is uniquely associated with an afterlife. Its elusive nature gave rise to those great organized clergies who claimed possession of a knowledge of salvation through their interpretation of scripture that usually they alone could read. The gnostic can go it alone, without clergy, and arrive now. In this sense the pervasive ideas of Plato and the Neoplatonists, who offer us metaphors and allegories of immediate mystical salvation, seems to be the common stuff that links all the diverse eruptions of gnosticism.

Gnosis, meaning "knowledge," becomes the quest of those competing sects, deriving from diverse sources, who have been called the gnostics. When, through Plato, Socrates declares, "Know yourself,"[1] one tenet of gnosticism was born. But much earlier, in the Hebrew Bible, Eve chose the fruit of gnosis from the tree and is treated thereafter—as is woman—as the flawed, outsider heretic in the Judeo-Christian-Islamic family of religions. Conversely, among the gnostics she is praised for her courage to choose knowledge rather than innocence (ignorance) and to defy the authority of the creator god of earth and people, who guards knowledge as his own. Eve is the hero of the light and the Promethean liberator from god's tyrannical authority. In Genesis and in later gnostic myth (such as the Origin of the World and the Reality of the Rulers), Eve is the mythical mother of gnosticism.

In Mesopotamia and along the Mediterranean, all the way from

Alexandria to Rome, from about 200 B.C.E. to 200 C.E., we witness a rich ferment of spiritual movements, all seeking answers to the enigmas of existence. This is the intertestamental period, in which appear most of the noncanonical apocrypha and pseudepigrapha, the Dead Sea Scrolls of the Essenes and the Corpus Hermeticum of Egypt. In this period of the mystery religion, messianic charismatic, philosopher, theologian, and mystic also fashioned those systems of wisdom sayings, doctrines, and myth, often recorded on scrolls, that have been classified as gnostic scripture. But until the twentieth century this gnostic scripture survived only as disparate fragments in Greek, Latin, Syriac, Coptic, old Persian, and even Chinese, along with a few major works in Greek and Syriac, notably the pagan Corpus Hermeticum, dating from the second and third centuries, which includes Poimandres, attributed to Hermes Trismegistos, and the Songs of Solomon, a book of gnostic psalms. For many generations of scholars and seekers, knowledge of gnosticism came primarily from the works of early church fathers, whose writings, even when fairly reliable in terms of stating gnostic tenets, were composed as fiercely unsympathetic refutations of gnosticism. Then in 1945 in the sands of Egypt was found the Nag Hammadi library, consisting of the great treasure of fourth-century translations into Coptic of earlier Greek texts. These fifty-plus documents constitute a bible of classical gnosticism.

Among modern scholars who have had their say about gnostic parentage, Bentley Layton, in *The Gnostic Scriptures,* sensibly sees gnosticism rooted primarily in classical Sethian philosophers, but he also speaks of the gnostic presence in the Greek-speaking synagogues and in early Christianity (notably in Simon Magus, Acts 8:9–12). The leading scholar of Jewish mysticism and Kabbalah, Gershom Sholem, looks to a Jewish origin of gnostic notions in his *Jewish Gnosticism, Merkabah Mysticism,* and *Talmudic Tradition,* and his near contemporary, Hans Jonas (gnosticism's first major interpreter), asserts that gnosticism began in radical circles in Samaria. The Italian historian Giovanni Filoramo notes that "many scholars propose a

Jewish origin for Gnosticism," and that the Nag Hammadi gnostic texts confirm a Jewish influence, yet he finds the whole Jewish thesis shaky, for lack of corroborating scripture.[2] Yet some major corroborating scriptures strengthen a Jewish thesis of origin: the Book of Baruch of Justin, the Secret Book of John, and parts of the Gospel of John. The Book of Baruch is primarily a Jewish-gnostic text (Baruch is an angel of Elohim), with Christian and pagan main characters, including Moses, Jesus, and Hercules. It may be that Baruch in its earliest form was a purely Jewish scripture, and the extraordinary work we have now is a somewhat Christianized version redacted during the Christian-Jewish period. Even the Christianizing effort is tentative, since its ecumenical editors have generously acknowledged the pagan origins of gnosticism by bringing the god Hercules into the cast.

As for the views of early church fathers on the source of gnosticism, Irenaeus of Lyon, in his *Adversus haereses* ("Against Heresies"), excoriated both the followers of Alexandrian Valentinos as well as the heresiarch and magician Simon Magus, among many others. The church fathers "simply traced back the rise of Gnosis to the devil."[3] The gnostics returned the favor by making the god of the Old and New Testaments the demiurge—or more bluntly, the devil.

Not all the church fathers' polemics against the gnostics were uninformed, however. The Alexandrian fathers Clement (d. 215?) and Origen (185?–254?) were well informed and, to counter the readings of the Valentinian school of biblical scripture, developed their own hermeneutics, which were based on an allegorical reading of scripture.

But what most enraged early Christians about the gnostics was not only their unsympathetic portrait of the traditional creator god and the rivalry for dominion in this emerging religion—there were many serious heretical rival sects posing threats to primitive Christianity—but their rejection of the essential creed that in Jesus there existed two natures: the human and the divine. For the orthodox, Christ was at once man and god, and after suffering on the cross he was resurrected and ascended as the son of god to heaven.

The gnostics denied Christ's two natures of human and divine, and labeled his human semblance merely that—a semblance, not a reality. For them Jesus was a celestial body incapable of human misery. They shared the second-century docetic belief that during his life on earth, Christ was a divine phantom, who only seemed to inhabit a human body and to die on the cross.[4] Since Jesus Christ did not die a human death or a divine death, his resurrection and ascension to heaven never took place. Likewise, his lifetime ministries, miracles, and suffering were mere appearances. In the Nag Hammadi library's First Revelation of James, the exalted Christ straightens out a commiserating James after his crucifixion: "I am the one who was in me. Never have I experienced any kind of suffering."[5] As for those who thought they could cause him pain, we see Jesus laughing at his would-be tormentors: "I laughed at their ignorance."[6] In sum, most of the gnostic sects rejected the usual symbolic interpretation of "the word became flesh" (John 1:14) in which the word of god resided in Jesus, who was at once the holy word and a human being. These rejectionist ideas were an anathema to the church, and the gnostics and docetists were examined at length and denounced for their terrible heresies by Irenaeus of Lyon, the bishop Ignatius of Antioch, and Hippolytus and Clement of Alexandria.[7] Later the gnostics were condemned by Augustine, who knew gnosticism from the inside, since he had been a fervent Manichaean in his youth.

The church fathers were concerned. Here we have the earthly Jewish messiah of Isaiah, who in the gospels becomes salvific Jesus, turned by the gnostics into a divinity who resembles an angel but is neither man nor god. And above Jesus is the gnostic god of light at odds with his rival, the ignorant god of the Bible. The creator god of the Bible has earned his title of darkness by creating man and woman as a prison containing the divine particles of light that fell from the pleroma, the fullness (the highest principle in the gnostic theogony). While the biblical god made light, that external light is a temporal illusion. True light is in the human spirit. The gnostic earned the title of illumination by seeking the inner light. And to know and become these particles of light though gnosis is to disappear into eternity. Clearly, the gnostics were heretics. They could become light or god—or whatever one calls the divine principle—in their own person, and without need of the angry church that saw them as evil and would eventually annihilate them.

The Jewish Moment at the Beginning of Gnosticism

One of the intriguing hypotheses about why and how gnosticism developed remains the earlier-noted Jewish one as described by Scholem and Grant. Grant suggests that the earliest gnostics operated in the first century before the Common Era as a turn elsewhere or inward by Jews disappointed that their foretold messiah had not come.

It must be remembered that the faces of Judaism, like that of the rabbi Jesus, were also changing and multiple. They changed again with each new interpreter, and their scriptures changed according to the eyes of each interpreter. Among those changing faces, whom Scholem, Grant, and others describe, were the Jewish gnostics who, as noted, were to give us the earliest extant gnostic scripture, the Book of Baruch.

The Book of Baruch attributed to Justin, preserved only as a paraphrase in Hippolytus's Refutation of All Heresies, represents one of the earliest stages of gnostic evolution. Grant calls it "an example of a gnosis almost purely Jewish . . . which owes its origin to three principles, two male and one female."[8] It contains a fascinating mixture of traditions, in which the first male is Hellenic Priapos, father of the cosmos, while Jewish Elohim is father of this world and a lover of Edem (Eden), the female principle. Elohim breathes spirit into Adam, while Edem breathes soul into the first man. Baruch ("blessed" in Hebrew) is the tree of life and the chief angel. Naas, the serpent, is the tree of the knowledge of good and evil and the chief maternal angel. Eden is many: garden, earth, Israel, a symbol of Eve, and the earth mother. In later speculations the unknown god in his various guises has a male and female element and is called the mother-father of us all, or god with a female principle or emanation. The female emanation is usually Sophia, who is wisdom. Because of a disturbance and inadequacy in god, she is separated from him, falls from the pleroma, and creates the world. In referring back to Christian gnosticism's Jewish origin and early ties between gnosticism and early and late Kabbalah, Grant observes that Justin's variation of Judaism "is like the mystical Judaism we find in the [medieval Spanish] Zohar, where Yahweh is called the father and Elohim the mother."[9]

Despair and Turn to Light

The calamitous Roman occupation of Israel surely influenced the Jewish turn to gnosticism. After the failure of the Jewish rebellion in Jerusalem (66–70 C.E.), the misery of the Jews increased with the destruction of the Second Temple (70 C.E.). The utter failure of god to intervene on their behalf dashed their apocalyptic hopes for external help and opened a way to gnosticism. Grant describes the mess of destruction and despair: "For all practical purposes, the Gnostics must have been ex-Jews, renegades from their religion, for they had abandoned the deity of the Creator."[10] While the destruction of the Temple and the city of Jerusalem devastated and exiled the Jews, the later Christian Jews who composed the gospels turned that historic horror into a punishment for those Jews who failed to recognize their messiah and a reward and hope for those who did. In reality both Jews and Christian Jews were slaughtered and driven out of the razed city. This diaspora led to the spread of both gnosticism and Christianity. With Christian Judaism now in the gentile world, the new sect's laws of the Sabbath, circumcision, and diet were quickly altered, making large-scale conversion to Christianity a popular possibility. At the same time the original persecution and calamity, having been experienced equally by Jew and Christian Jew, led many to a gnostic solution, which is seen in the sudden eruption of gnosticism in all the new Christian terrains.

Rather than pinning hope on clergy and traditional places of worship, these heterodox Jews as well as Christian Jews chose to look for a light inside. For the gnostic that light is spirit, and its contemplation can lead to a knowledge of god, or even for one to adhere to or be god within oneself.[11] Then the body is left behind, and escape is possible from earthly time through the inner light. To know that light of being signifies escape from temporal and bodily captivity on the material earth and a return to origin, to the precinct of eternal light from which the spark of the spirit came.

In the religions of the world the escape from ordinary time and matter, through the mind, into an extraordinary dimension of spirit and revelation has come under the label of mysticism.

Nature of the Mystical Leap

Mysticism is a phenomenon appearing in many forms, in east and west and in all continents, and each religious sect carries its own terminology to describe it. Sometimes it is regulated by shamans or carried out as a personal heterodoxy at the fringes of an established religion (Paracelsus, Teresa of Avila, Boehme). Sometimes it is at the heart of the creed itself, which may be said of Buddhism, gnosticism, or ancient Hasidism and later Kabbalah. The mystical instant may be called illumination or extinction through *nirvana,* or the light following the annihilation of annihilation. The Persian Sufis call it a conference of birds and the Japanese Zen Buddhists *satori.* The process itself takes on many descriptive metaphors, such as "the four levels of cognition" in Plato, "the negative way" in Pseudo-Dionysios and John of the Cross, and "the steps of the ladder" in Philo and again John of the Cross. Each rung of the ladder may signify darkness, illumination, and union that is an ineffable ecstasy of oblivion. These various steps usually suggest a cosmic ascent from sensations of the body through the soul to the light and loss of earthly consciousness. The ascender dies from ordinary time on the way to the source of spirit. Then the major question is with what or with whom is the union. With god? A pantheistic all? A Buddhist void? A Plotinian One? A gnostic particle of light? But perhaps the most obscure question in mysticism is the nature of that union. The two essential but discrete types of union are the monistic and the theistic.

If god is postulated as the universal principle to be reached at the end of ascent, then the monistic mystic seeks identity with god and total immersion in god, while the theistic mystic seeks a communion with or adhesion to god, but no loss of personal identity. In monism subject and object become one; the mystic is absorbed into the deity—Saint Teresa speaks of a drop falling into a river—and thereby achieves union (*enosis*) and divinization (*theosis*). Monism is typically Neoplatonic and Christian. John of the Cross (Juan de la Cruz) seeks self-abolition, being lost in god, one with god, and with one identity, god. The most common Christian gnostic articulation of mystical experience is the monistic model, where one moves from initial unknowing (the *agnosia* of darkness and error, as opposed to *gnosis*) to full illumination and total union. The notion of being deified, of passing into and becoming the light, is found in Plotinos, whose "one becomes the One," and similarly in the writings attributed to the pagan gnostic Hermes Trismegistos. In Hermes the soul rises on an ascending scale of mental states though the spheres. Hans Jonas describes the journey of the self, while still in the body, which attains "the Absolute as an imminent, if temporary, condition." In that instant, with a translation of "objective stages into subjective phases of self-performable experience whose culmination has the form of ecstasis, gnostic myth has passed into mysticism (Neoplatonic and monastic), and in this new medium it [the attainment of the Absolute] lives on long after the disappearance of the original mythological beliefs."[12]

By contrast with Platonist mystical fusion and oneness, Martin Buber in *I and Thou* rejects the monistic notion of "I am god." For the theist the notion of becoming the godhead is shameful and deprives the creator of independent existence. Theistic mysticism—characteristic of the Bible, Jewish gnosticism, the Kabbalist Zohar, and a majority of postmedieval seekers—holds to an ultimate separation of the human and the divine. As Scholem states, the Jewish mystic "retains a sense of distance between the Creator and His creature."[13] This dualism of person and god is frequently symbolized in the *merkabah*, the divine throne-chariot that carries the soul skyward to god, which is illuminated by god's presence but does not disappear into and become god. There is the ascent, adhesion but not the fusion.

Ascension during One's Life to the Eternal

The gnostics developed their own lexicon to map the experience of self-knowledge, which drew on the philosophical speech of Alexandrian Platonism as well as the mythologies of the Bible and of classical Greek and Egyptian antiquity. From these sources they formed their own cosmogony (creation of the world) and theogony (creation of the gods) and their fantastic symbolic legends.

While confined to the earth, the gnostics believed, each human being consists of a vital trinity of material body, temporal soul, and eternal spirit. Within that physical and mental trinity, one is free to ascend from body and soul to eternal spirit, even before death, from darkness to the freedom of full illumination. These powerful, radical ideas opened interior ways of endless possibility. Nothing is all new, yet the specific articulation of gnosticism was a new, alluring alternative to the normative religion that locked ideas into dogma, bureaucracy, and worldly power to defeat infidels and banish creative solitude. The attractive equation of knowledge, light, spirit, and god was at the heart of gnosticism as it developed in differing modes all over the ancient world.

Around the time of the crucifixion, gnosticism rose in the Near East, Egypt, and the European Roman Empire. In this turbulent period of diaspora, dispirit, intense speculation, and self-proclaimed prophets and messiahs, the gnostics chose the meditative gaze. Their dualism was not only of two conflicting gods but of external flesh and internal spirit, and these two human attributes lived in absolute separation. There is nothing new about the Cartesian split of mind and matter, but in the instance of the gnostics mind is all and the rest an encumbrance. The body is matter. Their turn from the body is not Asian asceticism or flesh-loathing puritanism. It is simply that mind is the only reality that can turn into light. In this sense we see how close the gnostics are to Plotinian immersion in the all, the sun, the good, where all the rest is illusion. In gnosticism (which Plotinos derided) the ascent is inward to the fullness, to a glimpse of and participation in the light of the pleroma. Other than the jargon and metaphor, there is little difference in the mystical leap to immediate salvation in gnosticism and the Plotinian way. Both offer salvation now in one's life, in contrast to the three orthodox Abrahamic religions, which hold out some form of salvation as a reward after death. The Kabbalist and Christian mystics, who have operated on the borders of heresy, also report ascension and adhesion to or immersion in god, and their voyage is immediate and presumably outside time. The meaning of their experience differs specifically from that of the gnostic, however, in that their communion or union with god is not consummated as a confirmation of eternal salvation—all that must occur as a reward in the afterlife—while the gnostic does find eternal salvation in the now, which even later death will not erase.[14] While this is not usually recognized, gnostic salvation now makes mortality not only secondary but also, as in the Judaism of the Torah, final, with no probability of afterlife or heaven. For the Torah-based Jews, however, reward is closeness to god and a good, virtuous, long life on earth; for the gnostics it is a flash of disappearance of the spirit from body and earth to return to the original light source, to become that light source or god or whatever name one attaches to the most significant creative principle, and then to return to earth, body and soul, consoled by the knowledge of that glimpse and participation.

Jewish, Christian, and Gnostic Gods

In Judaism god is the principal force, and Satan (meaning "adversary") is a scarcely mentioned member of god's court (Job 1–2 and Zechariah 3:1–2). He is god's enforcer among humans, and only in 1 Chronicles 21:1 is there ambiguity as to whether he is an adversary of god or of humans. In this one instance of possible evil and opposition, he is at worst a minor digression. Judaism is not dualistic with regard to divine powers, and apart from the early rival Canaanite gods of the Torah, god has no rival within the ranks of Jewish divinities.

In contrast to the feeble Satan of Judaism and the fearful devil of the later Christians comes the gnostic demiurge, who is no other than the great and good creator god of the Bible,[15] now operating demonically down in the realm of sinister evil. While the creator god loses virtue, he remains almighty, for it is he who created the world. With his command "Let there be light" (the light of illusion), Eve and Adam were trapped on earth, and god becomes the warden of their human spirit.

By these shifts of power and province, the attributes of the Judeo-Christian god are divided between the two polar gods. There is the god of spirit, whose attributes are light and knowledge, and the god of matter, whose attributes are darkness and error. In varying texts, from China to western Europe, Yahweh takes on nasty and fearful-sounding names, such as Yaldabaoth, Sakla, and Samael. Like fallen Lucifer, he is the boss and patron of evil, whose main business occurs on his creations, the earth under its revolving sun star.

Replacing the creator god of illusion at the top is the interior god of light whose domain is everywhere there is mind. The earthbound are not pure matter and darkness, which should be seen as impediments to transcendence, but also particles of light, which are reached not through the church or the outer firmament but through meditation. The inner god of light represents the hope of return.

Clearly, the gnostics turned Judeo-Christian theology upside down. They had the audacity to make Yahweh into a vain creator of the earth and its imprisoned inhabitants and, in many scriptures, simply into the devil. This extreme turnaround must be understood in the historic complexity of gnostic rivalry with Christian orthodoxy and the need of each sect to hide its ancestry. The earliest Christians were Jews. Yet in slipping away from Judaism, Christianity demonized the Jews. Ultimately, that Jewish earthly messiah will be in the name of Jesus Christ (Yeshua Mashiah), the foremost god, the immediate god, clearly replacing the Hebrew Bible deity and, in practice and in popular understanding, god himself. While in the gospels Jesus will sit to the right of god's throne, in popular thought and iconography god and salvation are more understood through Jesus. The tripartite nature of god explains away this popular misunderstanding, but the perception persists that Jesus is not only god but also, for all practical purposes, the immediate god to address in prayer.

If the Christian god must share his realm of significance with Jesus and to a much lesser extent with the holy spirit, then the gnostics carry sectarian rivalry with an ancestral father religion in the Hebrew Bible radically further. The gnostics deconstruct both Judaism and Christianity and reconstitute them both to conform to their own creation myths. In both Christian and gnostic reconstruction of precursors, however, these ritual killings of the founding father contain astonishing inconsistencies. The Christians demonize the Jews but exempt all the early Christians, who were also Jews, by ignoring or dissembling their religious identity as Jews. While the gnostics demonize the original god of the Jews, they pay less attention to the Jews themselves, who are seldom mentioned—though they are not well treated when they are mentioned. Classical gnosticism sees the creator god of the Bible not only as the god of the Jews but principally as the demiurgical tyrant of misguided Christians, who have appropriated and interpreted the Hebrew Bible as their own Christian Bible. And insofar as Christians worship that biblical god, they also obey the demon of darkness. But the misguided Christians have a way out. They can become true Christians if, as Christian gnostics, they renounce the god of the Bible and turn to the invisible father of all.

Jesus among the Gnostics

How does Jesus fit into this revisionism? Among the Christian gnostics, Jesus is the mediating figure. He is often the envoy (or angel) of the invisible true father. This position makes him higher than a human, less than the godhead. He is normally monophysitic, which is to say that he is only spirit and his body on earth is illusion. He has no human body but only *appears* to have died on the cross. In his highest position as envoy, he appears as an eternal being (an aeon) sent to earth to instruct humans in the ways of light and redemption.

While the Christian gnostics, including the later Cathars, claim that their Jesus is the true Jesus, he is so different from the Jesus of orthodox Rome and Byzantium as to make his gnostic articulation impossible for Christians to accept.

Pagan Gnostics

There were also classical gnostics who did not derive from Judaism or Christianity. These were the pagan gnostics. Largely in Alexandria, they adapted Neoplatonism and local Hermetic mystery religion into a new mythical dualism in which flesh is dark temporal matter while mind (*nous*) is knowledge and sunlike. Knowledge will make us better than the gods, for once we have acquired it we are both mortal and immortal. The pagans believed that the great Hermetic philosopher is Hermes Trismegistos (the thrice-greatest), who sprang from the Egyptian god Thoth and Greek Hermes. In Poimandres (Shepherd), a superb literary tractate attributed to this Hermes, he gives his severely dualistic view of the cosmos, expressed as visionary experience. The demiurge is the maker who originally emanates from the androgynous father of all. The maker makes humans, whom he sets in the prison of the material earth. But an androgynous primal person (*anthropos*) descends to earth and mingles with the cosmos, offering spiritual promise. He carries in him a spark of holy light. The human creature, by the act of gnosis in his or her life, can rise from the body through interior light to join the light-body of god.

Zoroastrianism, a Precursor of Gnosticism

Among these diverse sources of gnosticism, Iranian Zoroastrianism (Mazdaism) had a paramount influence in eastern gnosticism. While it did not directly reach the earlier Syrian-Egyptian gnostics, Zoroastrian structure and notions of salvation profoundly affected third-century Mani and Manichaeism. Led by Ahura Mazda, the Zoroastrian good spirits (*ahuras*) contend against dark evil spirits (*daevas* or *divs*), led by Ahriman, for the fate of the human soul. The people of light are pitted against the people of darkness. When Mazda (meaning "wise") wins, the soul ascends to the realm of light. Particularly during the sixth-century B.C.E. Babylonian captivity, when Jews were in a region where Zoroastrianism was practiced, this dualistic religion also affected Judaism. There is obviously a coincidence of idea and word in the Essenes of the Manual of Discipline, with their sons of light warring against the sons of darkness. The Iranian dualism coincides with the essential character of the gnostic speculation, which emerges as a system of antinomies.

Gnostics as Enlightened Christians

The majority of gnostics saw themselves as the enlightened Christians, at least in the first periods of their growth. By the end of the second century of the Common Era, while traditional Christianity was becoming a powerful independent religion, the gnostics were converting and spreading in great numbers and across many borders of Asia, Africa, and Europe. To convert traditional Christians to their intelligence, the gnostic philosophers developed an allegorical exegesis of the gospels to prove that Christian gospel revealed gnostic truths. They produced the first theological Christian literature, and in the second century their writings were apparently significantly more extensive than those of the Catholic and Orthodox churches.[16] Their favored text to comment on was the Gospel of John (compare Herakleon), which they treated as their gospel. In the first lines of the Gospel, John establishes the notion of the essential interior light and tells the role of John the baptizer:

> He was not the light.
> but came to testify about the light.
> The light was the true light
> which illuminates every person
> who comes into the world. (John 1:8–9)

The high clergy in Rome, Antioch, and Constantinople was alarmed. Not only were the gnostics converting newcomers by appropriating the gospels as their own, but they were also converting Christians to their heresy and spreading from land to land as an unquenchable fire. These gnostics seemed to turn every sacred notion on its head, from Eve, who could be seen as virtuous for choosing knowledge, to the creator god, who was denigrated as proud, legalistic, and ignorant and assigned the lowest demonic place in the cosmic hierarchy. In those ostensibly Christian schools of the gnostics, especially pernicious were the intellectual and mystical notions of Alexandrian Valentinos (Valentinus), Basilides, and the Sethians, which, from at least 135 to 450, were prominent. To the initially decentralized networks of the early Christians, these were formidable heretics. These Alexandrians, along with Mani and his followers, were reviled and furiously opposed as usurpers of their salvific terrain. By the end of the fifth century, the heterodox sects were in large part muted. However, as late as

Saint Augustine (354–430), the battle of numbers for possession of the Christian heart lingered. An emblem of those times is Augustine's protean persuasions, the gnostic who saw the light of Christianity. Though later he wrote abundantly against the gnostics, early in his career the theologian was a fervently active and roaming gnostic in Italy and North Africa, one who proselytized and preached the message of Manichaeism. His *Against Faustus*, in which he denounces his former Manichaean master Faustus, is one of many important works, along with those by Irenaeus, Hippolytus, Origen, Epiphanius, and Tertullian, that summarize and refute the gnostic heresy.

In response to these many challenges to the church, Christian apologists forcefully rejected "the abominable writings of the demonic heretics." Ironically, in the course of angry refutation, the heresiologists imitated the gnostic philosophers and developed their own Christian exegesis. For its part, gnosticism with immense vitality challenged and widely subverted Christian theology—which had its own divisions—and remained Christianity's most serious rival, even when muted, until the birth of Islam.

The Destruction of Rival Gnostics and Classical Civilization

Christianity responded to rivals of their dominion by silencing the gnostics along with the religious and philosophical remnants of the Greco-Roman world. As early as the second century, Christian clerics destroyed gnostic texts, burned meeting places, and went after the pagan arts and philosophers with a fury. But how did the syncretistic Hellenistic ethos disappear in the west? The classical Greek civilization of Alexandria had given us Euclid and his principles of geometry, Longinos describing Sappho's religious ecstasy in "On the Sublime," the philosophers Philo and Plotinos keeping Platonism alive, and the main schools of classical gnosticism. But after this great flowering, the city's culture was violently shut down. Christians under

the command of the Alexandrian patriarch Theophilos of Alexandria
(later saint), with approval by the Byzantine emperor Theodosios
I, leveled the major temple complex of the Sarapeum in 391. In the
Sarapeum was lodged the Mouseion (museum) library, the greatest
library of antiquity, holding about 700,000 rolls. After razing the
buildings, Theophilos used the temple stone to construct Christian
churches. His nephew Bishop Cyril (later saint), attacked Egyptian
Christian and Hermetic gnostics as heretics, burned synagogues,
and drove the Jews out of Alexandria. In 415 Cyril ordered a mob of
Nitrian monks to stone to death the woman philosopher, astronomer,
and mathematician Hypatia, the last major Platonist in Alexandria.[17]
In Constantinople the bishop went after the Nestorian and Arianist
orders. All perceived rivals of the church were slaughtered—classical
Neoplatonists, Christian and pagan gnostics, and Jews, as well as the
"heretical" orders within the Christian compass.

When Christianity became the state religion of the Roman
Empire, there seemed a chance for religious and political stability in
Christendom. The Christians were no longer persecuted by Rome.
Rather, a new theocracy set out to combat heretics within the empire,
and the war against the gnostics was waged from the top. The long
campaign was only partially successful. Hellenism was in tatters, the
marble Roman gods of the pantheons crushed, and the parent religion
Judaism disenfranchised and insignificant, but the faith was still
caught up in doctrinal struggles. The foremost enemy remained the
great gnostic heresy. The gnostics in Alexandria were early on fiercely
persecuted by a church tolerated by Rome. When the Roman Empire
under Constantine became both the political as well as the religious
master of the ancient world, the destruction of the "acosmic heresy"
seemed to be nearly total. Christian clerics burned the writings of the
heretics. The light people buried many scrolls of their scripture, which
in at least one Egyptian site, at Nag Hammadi, was to be discovered
sixteen hundred years later. The gnostics themselves were killed
or hounded out of one place but would appear elsewhere, even in
Constantinople nearly a thousand years later as the Slav Bogomils,

and gnostic speculation would outlast the Roman Empire, the Eastern Roman Empire, and the Byzantine Empire.

A few gnostic texts survived, quoted at length in the diatribes of their accusers. But though Alexandria, North Africa, and Syria ceased being gnostic centers, the religion of light persisted in other areas, mainly remote ones: in western China, in pockets of Mesopotamia, and in the Balkans and southwestern Europe until well into the fifteenth century. But after repression by early Catholic heresy hunters and a Persian king, by later crusaders and inquisitors in France and Italy, and finally by conquering Mongol and Turkish armies, their light was put out and their dominion of influence a memory.[18]

Had Alexandria Triumphed

There followed centuries of silence. Gnostic texts were found beginning in the Italian renaissance, but only in the twentieth century did we come upon the equivalent of a Dead Sea Scrolls resurrection with the great find near the town of Nag Hammadi in Egypt, which afforded us texts to comprehend, for the first time, the literatures and thought of the gnostics. Jorge Luis Borges points out that it might not have been this way had history been different, favoring a gnostic majority. In an early essay, Borges spoke about the Alexandrian gnostic Basilides, whose work we still have only in fragmentary and corrupt form as bequeathed to us by his condemners. In "A Defense of Basilides the False" Borges writes, "Had Alexandria triumphed and not Rome, the extravagant and muddled stories that I have summarized here would be coherent, majestic, and perfectly ordinary." But Alexandria did not triumph. A philosopher of the knowledge of nonbeing and the abyss, Basilides was one of the most fascinating of the gnostic thinkers, but he is preserved only in the writings of his opponents, and their summaries contradict each other on significant points. That his works were not included in the Nag Hammadi library or in other finds is lamentable. Were we to uncover a major original text, on the basis of existing evidence, we would have the writings of an essential ancient philosopher. There is a strange fact of survival. We have abundant texts by two Neoplatonist philosophers from Alexandria—Philo, a Jew, and Plotinos, a pagan—yet no original text of their fellow Alexandrian philosopher Basilides. This strongly implies that to Christian apologists, the gnostics were held to be more dangerous than the Jews or the classical philosophers. So the gnostic writings of their greatest rival had to be destroyed. It is some comfort that at least their refutations in the works of Christians fathers, such as Irenaeus and Augustine, do exist and inform, if not satisfy, us.

A Resurfacing of Gnostic Communities

With the iconoclastic rage unleashed by Christian orthodoxy in Alexandria, Athens, Rome, and the Eastern Roman Empire against classical antiquity and the gnostic heresy, by the middle of the fifth century even the widespread gnostics began to fade. Western culture moved into its darkest centuries. Yet much light still shone at the eastern and western edges of Europe, in Byzantium on the east and Muslim Spain on the west, and especially among the more structured Manichaean gnostics, whose message of light survived with vigor. Within a century after Mani's death, in about 276, the founder's religion spread throughout the Roman Empire and Asia and was the sturdiest of the gnostic sects. Even after the earlier dismal suppression of other gnostic schools in North Africa and most of Europe, areas of ascetic Neomanichaeans survived largely beyond the grasp of pope and emperor or at the outer reaches of their dominion, from Turkestan to Carthage—in Persia, in the Arabic Near East, in western China, and in southern France, where persecution was initially less extreme. There were also the Islamic gnostics in central Asia. And there was the amazing trail of the Neomanichaean Paulicians, who from the sixth to the tenth centuries were in Armenia and the eastern provinces of the Byzantine Empire and who later merged with the Neomanichaean Bogomils, who were driven out of Constantinople and persisted in Syria and Armenia; it was Bogomil missionaries who in the eleventh century brought their form of Manichaeism to the Cathars in France. The Manichaeans in Chinese Turfan became the leaders of the state religion of the important Uigur empire in Turkestan, western China (762–840). In its territorial range, in its cultural multiplicity, no religion has been so internationally receptive as has gnosticism. Into its diversity of sects and scriptures it incorporated essential figures from the world's major philosophies and religions: Buddha, Plato, Ahura Mazda, Apollo, Moses, Jesus, and Muhammad.

The thirteenth century was tragic for the gnostic speculation, both in the Far and Middle East and in the European West. In Asia it was Genghis Khan's horsemen who from 1218 to 1224 stormed over the gnostics in Chinese Turkestan; in Provence it was Pope Innocent III's Albigensian crusade (1209) into southern France that cleansed the "Manichaean scourge of god" from the earth. The crusade was followed by a century of the newly formed Inquisition (1231). After another century of murder, torture, seizure of properties, and forced conversion, by the end of the fourteenth century the Cathars (or Albigensians), who flourished in the Occitan region in southwest France, were wiped out, their meditation extinct. Only small numbers of Cathar gnostics survive today, making up the Cathar church in parts of France and Canada.

Recovery of Gnostic Scriptures

By the end of the Middle Ages the long reconstruction of that gnostic memory was in full swing. A large collection of writings known as the Corpus Hermeticum (or the Hermetica), attributed to Hermes Trismegistos, was repeatedly copied. The central work of the Hermetica is the Poimandres, a Socratic dialogue between the dark body and the enlightened mind, or *nous,* whose purpose is the soul's escape and ascent.

Then in 1909 J. Rendel Harris discovered an old Syriac (Aramaic) manuscript of the Songs of Solomon comprising forty songs (originally forty-two; the first two are missing). These songs, carrying the false attribution to Solomon, are among the most beautiful and profound songs of world religious literature. Another long poem is the Song of the Pearl, contained in the apocryphal Acts of Thomas, a Syriac text that also exists in Greek. It is an extraordinary narrative of a prince who seeks a pearl in Egypt, which he finds, thereby bringing the soul from darkness into the kingdom of light. To these we must add, again from Egypt, the Coptic Songbook of Manichaean poems, as well as collections of Mandaean poems, songs, prayers, and narrative cosmologies that first came into Europe through Portuguese monks returning from Asia.

Despite these accumulating discoveries, the quilt of gnostic scriptures was thin. Because the destruction of the great ancient libraries and specifically of gnostic sacred texts was so complete, our knowledge of essential ideas of gnosticism still had to be detected from Christian writings against them. Then in 1945 in Egypt a farmer discovered near Nag Hammadi a buried cache of thirteen codices containing some fifty texts, in fourth-century Coptic translation from Greek second- and third-century compositions. After a few decades of hijinks, high adventure, and even the intervention of Carl Jung, these splendid texts were finally translated into French, German, Italian, and English under the title of the Nag Hammadi library.[19] Gnosticism had found a new voice. When the Dead Sea Scrolls were found on the west bank of the Dead Sea in 1947 near Wadi Qumran, suddenly a fringe sect of Essenes, opposed to Jerusalem, had abundant scripture from out of a vase. Similarly the gnostics, a religion on the fringe, but one that had extended from the east coast of China to the west coast of Portugal, came, after being concealed because of critical danger, into light. These two instants of discovery were supreme in the resurrection of an apparently extinguished body of thought.

Gnostic Stories and Terminology

Most of the gnostic texts have an engaging literary clarity. In these, abstraction yields to striking metaphor. One example is the unsurpassed allegorical adventure in the Song of the Pearl, or the divine orgy in the Origin of the World. In the latter, the romping creator god holds dominion over Eden as he chases and rapes the virgin Eve, who represents courage, defiance, and knowledge; as a result of an abominable gang rape by the creator god and his angelic aides, Eve begets generations of trapped demigod souls, who are our ancestors. But after the fiercely discrediting deeds by the demiurge, the mountains of the first father will blaze and fire will turn on its maker, who will burn inside the forests. Then "light will cover darkness." There are constants to these wild tales that slip in allegorically or emerge in plain description: a radical and alien stance to traditional creed; a mystical encounter with invisible spirit; and a flight from initial ignorance and darkness to silent freedom and light.

Other tales fare less well in transcription. Confusion is inevitable with so many schools, conflicting symbolism, and variation of a mythic story. Consider the common theme of the fall and enslavement of the soul in the body's prison and its longing for return to its source. What is that holy source? It has a babel of names: the androgynous god of light, god the father/god the mother, the Sethian unknowable god, the Valentinian father of truth, the Manichaean original light, the abyss of nonbeing that in Basilides means the demiurge. Often there is a mishmash of hierarchical names, titles, and abstractions, where the author appears seduced by the glory of language to the detriment of meaning and delight of scholars.

Gnostic Despair and Inner Light, and the Emergence of a Self-centered Religion

From the gnostics' very inception, their inner light came as a response to oppression and dismay. The circumstance of despair with the material world that impelled their original alienated vision as well as their turn inward to dissident knowledge and meditation probably had its beginnings with first-century Jews who were shaken by the destruction of their temple in Jerusalem and the forced diaspora into neighboring lands. With their apocalyptic vision and hope arrested by exile and the failure of god to halt Roman armies and their endless crucifixions, some Jews from Palestine and Alexandria turned from faith in the outside creator god to a revelatory knowledge attained in solitude. A similar dashing of apocalyptic hope also stirred early Christians who were finding their way and from whose ranks was to come the main body of converts to gnosticism.

From these multiple strands of Jewish and Christian hopelessness and from Hermeticism in Egypt, mythical theologies in Babylonia, and Zoroastrian dualisms in Persia came a new self-centered religion, based no longer on the creator god of the Jewish Bible but on imaginative forces of mind seeking a personal awakening of the spirit to light. It is imperative to remember that gnostics distinguish between soul and spirit. Spirit is higher, also associated with breath (*pneuma*), while soul is still hylic, that is, connected to body and the earth, dependent on their form but capable, through gnosis, of rising to the salvific level of spirit.

In the notion of a self-centered religion we have the essence of gnosticism's most radical contribution to the history of ideas. There is no longer only a social contract between god and humans in which obedience to the master god is virtue. Now the *self* is valuable. The self may become divine. The self may become god. Such flouting of authority is of course suppressed as heresy. To understand this universal push by the gnostics toward self-realization, we may remember the sixth-century B.C.E. pre-Socratic philosopher Herakleitos, exiled for his radical disagreements with his native Ephesos, one of whose surviving sayings centers the search for mind in "I looked for me."

Consider the rationalist lens grinder from the Amsterdam ghetto Baruch Spinoza (1623–77), whose central ideas pronounce the words of discordant gnosis. In his day he could not say that the creator god did not exist. He said something equally radical, which he conveyed by correspondence to Leibnitz and other philosopher friends, which is that the universe is a single substance capable of an infinity of attributes, including physical extension and thought. God is not the creator of nature beyond himself. God is nature in its fullness, its *plenum* (Latin for the Greek *pleroma* of the gnostics). In Spinoza's ethical system the intellect is active and escapes earthly desires through knowledge, *scientia* (Latin for *gnosis*). A human is equal to god because all is god, which is understood in solitude by the active intellect. For his ideas, and for his higher criticism of the Jewish Bible, which he was translating, he was early excommunicated (1656), and his blasphemous pantheism could not be published during his lifetime.

Elaine Pagels speaks of the gnostics' independence from the authority of orthodox religion and of god, and of god's divinity, which can be, through knowledge, found within us. She writes, "Orthodox Jews and Christians insist that a chasm separates humanity from its creator: God is wholly other. But some of the gnostics who wrote these gospels contradict this: self-knowledge is knowledge of God; the self and the divine are identical."[20]

In the Gospel of Thomas, a gnostic Jesus (in parabolic words resembling a Daoist saying or a Zen koan) states that while the orthodox leaders separate humans from god's heaven by placing it outside and up in the sky, god and his realm are actually inside us and everywhere outside. In the pantheism of the living Jesus, god's realm and self are identical and everywhere:

> If your leaders tell you, "Look, the kingdom is in heaven,"
> then the birds of heaven will precede you.
> If they say to you, "It's in the sea,"
> then the fish will precede you.
> But the kingdom is inside you and it is outside you.

While early Christianity was replete with conflicting creeds and many gospels circulating and competing for authority and a place in the canon, including the Gospel of Thomas, the Gospel of Mary, the Gospel of Philip, the Gospel of Truth, and the Book of Thomas, the church fathers were seeking to squelch secret teachings and dissent from an emerging canon. And despite a later sentimental view that early Christians had a unanimity of belief and charitable tolerance of outsiders, the times were intensely dangerous for dissenting Christians and especially for gnostic Christians. In comparing the dissidence of John the baptizer with that of gnostic revolutionaries in those divisive times, James M. Robinson, the editor of *The Nag Hammadi Library in English,* observes that as the ingredients of Christianity coalesced and became a set doctrine, the followers of the radical Christian Jews soon became powerful, comfortable, and conventional and took on the "basic stance . . . of the myopic heresy-hunters."[21] As for the gnostics, they in turn appeared to abandon traditional god and church for a personal mythopoeia to accompany, in image and word, their turn inward. Robinson writes,

> [Their] outlook on life increasingly darkened; the very origin of the world was attributed to a terrible fault, and evil was given status as the ultimate ruler of the world, not just a usurpation of authority. Hence the only hope seemed to reside in escape. Because humans, or at least some humans, are at heart not the product of such an absurd system, but by their very nature belong to the ultimate. Their plight is that they have been duped and lured into the trap of trying to be content in the impossible world, alienated from their true home. And for some, concentrated inwardness undistracted by external factors came to be the only way to attain repose, the overview, the merger into the all which is the destiny of one's spark of the divine.[22]

These rebels, trying to make sense of the trap of an impossible world and move from alienation to a divine spark, were, as were so many, influenced by Platonic thought. They were affected by both Plato and Platonism, in the writings of Philo, and Greek revelation-wisdom texts from Egypt, in the Corpus Hermeticum. Other sources were Jewish mysticism as elaborated by Scholem in *Jewish Merkabah Mysticism and Talmudic Tradition* and the mysterious "Fourth Gospel" of John. The prologue of the book of John, "In the beginning was the word," gave gnostics a concordance with Genesis, the philosopher's logos, and platonic light. The Sethian texts carried on the Essene "antithesis of light and darkness, truth and lie, a dualism that ultimately went back to Persian dualism."[23] Of this turbulent and creative moment, where heterodoxy and disappointment seemed everywhere, Robert M. Grant wrote about a self-centered religion: "In the period when gnosticism arose, apocalyptic-minded Jews might have sought signs of the creator's power and his intervention on their behalf; philosophically minded Greeks might have looked for speculative wisdom, more or less rational in nature; but the gnostic preached himself and his true spiritual origin, both of which he had come to know by revelation."[24]

So after the late first century through at least the fourteenth and fifteenth centuries, in Northern Africa and virtually all of Europe, and from Asian Syria to Chinese Turkestan, gnostics were writing books of spiritual search and illumination that made self-knowledge a virtue rather than a sin. In the Origin of the World, Eve herself is not the servant of a devil snake who leads her to original sin. Rather, she is the primal heroine of self-knowledge. She also ceases to be a mere rib taken from Adam but his creator. By breathing spirit into the mouth of an inert clay figure of Adam on the ground, she gives life to the first man. As for the conniving snake, he is no longer a disguised devil but a luminous god who helps Eve snatch gnosis from the demiurge. In freeing Eve from shame and abuse, the gnostics—alone among major faiths—made woman an equal.

Revival in the Works of Dissident Philosophers and Poets

After its centuries of flourishing growth and then its virtual obliteration, gnosticism in the West found its true revival in the works of dissident poets, playwrights, philosophers, alchemists, and scientists. Traces of gnostic knowledge were basic to intellectual history. The Swiss physician and alchemist Paracelsus (1493?–1541) was the first modern doctor of chemical medicines and was also a student of gnostic thought. As an alchemist he sought to purify and transform nature's elements, freeing them of their low level of matter, so that nature in its purest forms could be used for curing the body and mind. In the Italian renaissance the Poimandres was popularly published by Lorenzo de Medici and later absorbed into the writings of the philosopher Giordano Bruno (1548–1600), who for his opposition to traditional Catholicism and his "cosmic theory of deity" was accused of gnostic perversions, among other heresies, and burned at the stake in the Piazza dei Fiori. The German mystic Jakob Boehme (1575–1624) was imbued with gnosticism. In his work he spoke of the blemished but ever creating Sophia who fell from the pleroma (Valentinos), the seven divine source spirits (Basilides' seven cosmic spheres), god as nothingness (Basilides' nonexistent god), and god as abyss (Valentinos).

William Blake (1758–1827) is the only writer in English letters to create his own complex gnostic system. His cranky and enlightened anger against clerical orthodoxy runs throughout the early *Songs of Innocence and Experience.* It is in his long prophetic poems, however, that Blake ventures fully into gnostic cosmogonies and theogonies. The god of Reason in *The Book of Urizen* recounts how in the prison of earth the mind is captive and has been deprived of eternity and light:

> Forgetfulness, dumbness, necessity!
> In chains of the mind locked up,
> Like fetters of ice shrinking together
> Disorganized, rent from eternity.

In Goethe we find this mocker of convention and religion choosing Faust as his wayward hero (Saint Augustine's Manichaean teacher was Faustus) and retelling the Manichaean myth of the messenger and his distracting but redemptive angels. In a fantastic cosmos, Faust's soul is, at the end, appropriately rescued from error and flown off to the realm of light.

The writer of gnostic themes, seeking inner knowledge in a condemned world, persists widely into more recent times. Herman Melville's "Fragments of a Lost Gnostic Poem" uses the words *fragment* and *lost* in the title to bespeak the sad paucity in his day of original gnostic texts. Melville's allegorical white whale may be seen as the monster of evil out of a gnostic dualistic bestiary, while his alien figure Ishmael, an orphan tossed on a hostile ocean, seeks knowledge of redemption as he clings to the wreckage of survival. The gnostic revival in literature and philosophy is found in Nietzsche's nihilism and the alienated hero of his *Thus Spake Zarathustra,* in Carl Jung's *Seven Sermons to the Dead,* and in the existentialist philosophers to whom Hans Jonas dedicates his chapter "Gnosticism, Nihilism, and Existentialism" in *The Gnostic Religion.*

To this list of modern gnostics who, having rejected orthodoxy and its creator god, chose acosmic solutions and transcendence, we can add many major figures, as Richard Smith does in his afterword to *The Nag Hammadi Library in English,* including "the good alien Superman battling forces of evil," whom Umberto Eco sees as clearly reflecting "Manichaean incontrovertibility"; Hermann Hesse's novels embodying the allegory of Jungian archetypes; and the alienated Beat Generation of Kerouac on the road and Ginsberg's outsider attack on convention as in his "Plutonian Ode," where he chants a fitful gnostic dirge, using Valentinian and Sethian epithets: "I salute you . . . Ialdabaoth, Aeon from Aeon born ignorant in an Abyss of Light." The leading contemporary critic Harold Bloom tells us in *The Anxiety of Influence* (1973) that authors must extinguish their literary fathers in order to find voyage. For Bloom the Kabbalah is his spiritual home, and Kabbalah's ally gnosticism is his "religion of belatedness."

The figure who everywhere shares qualities of gnosticism— probably by coincidence or knowledge of the unorthodox—is Franz Kafka. His castle is the domain of the unknowable god, and his climber antihero is, as in all of Kafka's novels, a humorous, depressed, skeptical orphan, without hope of fulfillment on earth, who must climb forever seeking, but not finding, an interior light that lies still concealed in dark error.

The Changing Face of Gnosticism

For many centuries "Manichaean" was an abusive term applied indiscriminately to all gnostic sects, and often to any dualistic heresy. But the Enlightenment—its very epithet means "entering light"— changed all that. It welcomed gnosticism as a powerful weapon against orthodoxy. It had its secular Voltaires and Humes who used a gnostic lexicon to trash conventional religion. For the irascible skeptic Hume, whose *An Enquiry into Human Understanding* (1748) by its name commends knowledge, religious convention was erroneous, dark, and ignorant. He summed up religion as "Stupidity, Christianity, and Ignorance." In that century, which had science and reason as well as Blake's "Self-annihilation & the grandeur of Inspiration" (Milton), Hume was simply drawing from an arsenal of gnostic charges to battle received tradition and its prevailing theologies.

For most of the last century, however, gnosticism may be seen not merely as a secret doctrine discovered by writers to bring the esoteric into their work or as an instrument to counter convention, but as a developing field with its own scriptures, increasing dramatically through archaeology and scholarship. Whatever its appellation, gnosticism is for real. It represents a world religion with fundamental notions and an extraordinary history. Today, gnosticism is surprisingly alive. Since the uncovering of the Nag Hammadi library in Egypt and the possession of a treasure of original gnostic scripture, gnosticism as an alternative intellectual and spiritual body of knowledge finds itself at a summit. This is evidenced in the quality of the historical and religious studies that gnosticism has generated, the many new translations of core scripture, and the general esteem and curiosity that gnosticism elicits, though in-depth knowledge of the history and nature of gnostic speculation is still rare. Apart from genuine coincidences in thought, gnosticism and Kabbalah find themselves in a similar period of revival and respect.

Contemporary interest in gnosticism is especially awake in France, where the Cathar past has become a pleasant obsession. The joy of free-spirited gnostic troubadours who sang of imperfect love as well as the massacres of a gnostic region capture the French and world imagination. The fortresses, castles, texts, and the Inquisition's city archives remain. The latter document some horrendous events in the years of the Cathar extermination, during which it is estimated that half the population of this dense region in southwestern France may have been killed. Historians, anthropologists, and novelists have turned their attention to the papal crusade in 1209, in which a northern French army of twenty thousand came down under the crusade commander Simon de Montfort and sacked the city of Béziers, slaughtering twenty thousand men, women, and children, including Cathar perfects and Catholic priests, indiscriminately, all for the possession of the rich lands of the south and a secure place in heaven. On one violent afternoon in 1308 in the mountain village of Montaillou, all the inhabitants who were not slaughtered were arrested. A bishop named Jacques Fournier was the inquisitor in the city of Pamiers who interrogated the surviving heretics. Some of those who confessed under torture were given penances, others went to the stake. (In 1320 in this same area, a center of Kabbalism, more than a hundred Jews—both forced converts wearing the yellow cross and professing Jews—were burned in mass.)[25] The Cathar incident took on greater meaning when in 1334 the inquisitor became Pope Benedict XII. Every word of his interrogations was stored in the Vatican. In the last years, after modern historians pressed the Vatican successfully for the publication of the *Fournier Register,* a slew of remarkable historical studies on the politics and religion of the Cathars have appeared. They include the classic *Montaillous: The Promised Land of Error* by Le Roy Ladurie, *The Perfect Heresy: Revolutionary Life and Death of the Medieval Cathars* (2000) by Stephen O'Shea, *The Cathars and the Albigensian Crusade* (2001) by Michael Costen, and a retelling of events revealed in the Fournier's interrogations, *The Good Men: A Novel of Heresy* (2002) by Charmaigne Craig, who traces three generations of a Montaillou family in her novel of misery, love, and trial within doomed walls.

The pained but extraordinary history of the gnostic speculation, with its external misadventures with church and civil powers that it rejected and its spirit-filled solitude of shining darkness, is every year a more articulate memory in books and images. The energy of discovery, as vital as that generated by archaeological and old temple finds, is apparent, from the Pays cathare (Cathar Land) signs that have popped up all over southern France to the growing band of serious thinkers and creative writers who have assumed the gnostic experience as their intellectual heritage.

Discovering the Book of the Mind

The gnostics endured. The many schools of gnosticism are of supreme interest. Now the loot at Nag Hammadi has given us works of Sethians as well as Valentinians, the latter including the Gospel of Truth, possibly by Valentinos himself. Other major finds from the Egyptian earth are the Gospel of Thomas, those wisdom sayings of Jesus that are now increasingly printed as and called the Fifth Gospel, and the non-Christian Sethian works the Three Steles of Seth, the Paraphrase of Shem, and Allogenes the Stranger. The Sethians, like the Essenes before the discovery of the Dead Sea Scrolls, were largely unknown except through commentators and opponents.

Whatever the school, there are general principles that go through all the gnostic teachings. We are confined to the earthly cycles of birth and death in a materialist universe, captive in the innermost dungeon that is the earth. We are remnants of spirit fallen into bodies, but bodies that retain a tiny element of salvation in them. That salvific hope is precisely the spark, the light of the spirit in the darkness of the flesh, but it remains unconscious and unknown until gnosis, a secret, revelatory knowledge, can extricate its light from cosmic involvement. Then, free of matter, the liberated spirit can rise and be reintegrated into the unknowable god.

Man and woman of the earth were originally eternal spirits, aeons, who fell tragically from the acosmic pleroma, the spiritual realm of light, into a cosmos of sensation where they are completely alien to their real being. Each spirit is invested in a decaying body. To escape from that declining flesh, the gnostic's gaze is directed inward to the spark, to the intuited mystery of the unconscious self that was once consubstantial with the unknown god. In this split of mind and body lies the conflictive dualism between spiritual good and material evil, and ultimately between the self and the planetary world, whose discord yields the human condition of alienation. Only knowledge (gnosis) of spiritual light—not faith prescribed by clergy—offers escape from the earthly dominion and return to the realm from which we have fallen.

Gnosis is a personal activity, and through reading, meditation, and search, its instant of appearance is probably as wordless as it is revelatory. Such is the nature of mystical experience, of ecstatic information, of epiphany wherever it is found—whatever previous information has been fed into the instant and however the ineffable is then translated back into speech, reason, or myth. In gnostic and other mystical meditations, there is a distinctive and different preparatory word, a darkness, illumination, and union, and after the oblivion of absence a new translation of the mystical experience for the world.

The gnostics were, like the Kabbalists, irredeemably bookish, and both engaged in elaborate mythology to map their transcendental journey. The Kabbalists even had god create the alphabet before creating the world so he would have speech to call the world into being. The gnostics were obsessed with recording the experience of gnosis and were prolific in creating, copying, and preserving libraries of scripture. Unfortunately, rival sects erased their books, just as they burned or obscured the heretical nine books of Sappho's poems to her ally, the god Aphrodite, or time and neglect effaced the music and number theory of the pre-Socratic philosopher Pythagoras. But now, with the existence and wide translation of the Nag Hammadi library of gnostic scriptures and other seminal texts from China to Mesopotamia, from Alexandria to Languedoc, we have at last an intimate garden with its tree of gnosis and a pleroma of writings detailing the gnostic word of return. We have the scriptures of a gnostic bible. Perhaps these books may generate another, preferable bible, without sect or text, without cipher or sound, which is the light in the book of the mind.

NOTES

Introduction

1. Throughout this book we have tried to avoid unnecessary capitalization of the word *god* and the names of personified spiritual powers and aeons. We are aware that the word *god* may be used as a name for the divine, but it frequently functions as a general term for the divine, so that even when *god* appears to be a name, it retains its primary nature as a term signifying the concept of divinity. For the same reason, other names of divine expressions, such as divine forethought, insight, and wisdom, are likewise left uncapitalized. Conversely, for the sake of clarity, when the Greek word *Sophia* is used for personified wisdom, that is capitalized, as are other names that are transliterated directly from other languages. We also want to avoid the common practice of singling out a particular deity, for example, the Judeo-Christian-Islamic deity, for the exclusive honor of the capitalized name "God," while other deities are relegated to the status of mere "gods" and "goddesses." We do not wish to limit the divine by restricting deity through name or selectivity. Traditionally the name and face of the divine are essentially unknowable, and so it is in this book.
2. See Barnstone and Meyer, *The Gnostic Bible.*
3. On the definition and classification of these texts, and the issue of terminology, see Barnstone and Meyer, *The Gnostic Bible;* King, *What Is Gnosticism?;* Layton, "Prolegomena to the Study of Ancient Gnosticism"; Marjanen, *Was There a Gnostic Religion?;* Meyer, *The Gnostic Discoveries;* Pearson, *Gnosticism and Christianity in Roman and Coptic Egypt;* and Williams, *Rethinking "Gnosticism."*

Chapter 1. The Gospel of Thomas

1. Coptic text: Nag Hammadi Codex II,2: 32,10–51,28. Greek fragments: Papyrus Oxyrhynchus 1, 654, 655. Quotations: Hippolytus, Refutation of All Heresies 5.7.20, 5.8.32.

2. Greek Papyrus Oxyrhynchus 654 adds, "and having ruled, you will rest" (partially restored).

3. Greek Papyrus Oxyrhynchus 654 reads, "it is under the earth."

4. Greek Papyrus Oxyrhynchus 654 adds, "and nothing buried that will not be raised" (partially restored).

5. Or, "Teacher" (Coptic *sah*), here and below.

6. Greek Papyrus Oxyrhynchus 1 has been reconstructed to read, "Where there are three, they are without god, and where there is only one, I say, I am with that one."

7. This phrase, "in the other ear" (Coptic *hᵉm pkemaaje*), may be an instance of dittography (that is, inadvertently writing something twice), or it may refer to another person's ear or perhaps one's own "inner" ear.

8. Greek Papyrus Oxyrhynchus 655 reads, "Do not worry, from morning to evening nor from evening to morning, either about your food, what you will eat, or about your clothing, what you will wear. You are much better than the lilies, which do not card or spin. And since you have one change of clothing, . . . you . . . ? (or, "And since you have no garment, what will you put on?") Who might add to your stature? That is the one who will give you your garment."

9. Or, "who has suffered."

10. Or, "That person is around the lamb," or "Why does that person carry around the lamb?"

11. The word *usurer* is partially restored. This word may be restored to read "a good person" (Coptic *ourome ᵉnchre[sto]s*), or "a usurer," "a creditor" (Coptic *ourome ᵉnchre[ste]s*), with very different implications. In the first instance a good person may be interpreted as the victim of violent tenant farmers, in the second instance (adopted here) an abusive creditor may be understood as opposed by the victimized poor.

12. Or, "Someone said" (Coptic *pejaf*). Sayings 73–75 most likely should be read as a small dialogue.

13. Partially restored.

14. Partially restored.

15. This statement of gender transformation differs from what is envisioned

in saying 22, where Jesus describes male and female becoming a single one. Saying 114 reflects a traditional ancient view that the female symbolizes what is earthly and mortal, as with the earth mother, and the male what is heavenly and divine, as with the heavenly father. Thus saying 114 seems to suggest that all people—men as well as women—who are earthly and mortal may be transformed to be with the divine and like the divine.

Chapter 2. The Gospel of Mary

1. Coptic text: Berlin Gnostic Codex 8502,1: 7,1–19,5. Greek fragments: Papyrus Oxyrhynchus 3525; Rylands Papyrus 463. The first six pages are missing from the Coptic manuscript, and the extant text begins in the middle of a dialogue between Jesus and his students on the nature of matter.
2. Or, perhaps, "rabbi," here and below (Coptic *joeis*).
3. Pages 11–14 are missing from the Coptic manuscript. The text resumes as Mary is recounting her vision of the ascent of the soul beyond the cosmic powers. The vision apparently described four stages of ascent, and these stages may have depicted the liberation of the soul from the four elements of this world, here described as expressions of cosmic evil and wickedness. The name of the first power is missing from the text, but it may have been "darkness," according to the list of the forms of the fourth power. The names of the other powers are "desire," "ignorance," and, apparently, "wrath," a deadly composite power. As in other texts relating to the career of the soul, the soul ascends through the realms of the powers and is interrogated by them. The soul is successful in her ascent from this world of matter and body, and she is set free at last.
4. This garment, which clothes the soul, is made up of all the features that characterize bodily existence in this world. The soul puts on this garment upon entering the world and removes it when leaving the world.
5. Or, "from," here and later in the sentence.

Chapter 3. The Gospel of Judas

1. Coptic text: Codex Tchacos 3: 33,1–58,29. Provisional translations of new papyrus fragments, published by Marvin Meyer and Gregor Wurst in the journal *Early Christianity* in 2010 (vol. 1), have been included in the translation.

2. Literally, "during eight days."

3. Or, "before his passion."

4. Or, "an apparition."

5. The land of Yehuda, Judea.

6. Or, "The god within you and his powers," or "The god within you and his servants" (partially restored).

7. Partially restored.

8. Restored. The reference here, with polemics directed against leaders of the emerging orthodox church, may rather be to an overseer (or bishop) or a minister (or deacon).

9. The following lines of translation are based on photographs of recovered fragments.

10. The reading and meaning of this line remain uncertain.

11. This teaching on stars assigned to people recalls the discussion in Plato, Timaeus 41d–42b, where it is stated that the creator of the world assigned each human soul to a star.

12. In Philo of Alexandria, *De Posteritate Caini* (On the Posterity and Exile of Cain), the name and character of Seth are linked to water, irrigation, and springs (noted by Birger A. Pearson).

13. Partially restored.

14. Or, "spirit," "demon." The role of Judas in the Gospel of Judas brings to mind features of Sophia, wisdom, in other gnostic texts. In the text entitled Pistis Sophia, Sophia is also referred to as a "spirit" or "demon" (*daimon, refšoor*), detained and persecuted in this world below and destined to return to the thirteenth aeon, her dwelling place and place of righteousness. Another author, who wrote under the name of Tertullian, likewise describes Sophia as a daimon (or *daemon,* in Latin). Irenaeus of Lyon mentions that in the second century, around the time the Gospel of Judas was being composed, there were some gnostics (Valentinians, Irenaeus suggests) who compared Judas and Sophia, and thought of Judas as "the type and image of that aeon (Sophia) who suffered."

15. Or, "a thatched roof."

16. The restoration and interpretation of this passage remains difficult.

17. Portions of the cosmology of the spirit are paralleled in such gnostic texts as the Secret Book of John, the Holy Book of the Great Invisible Spirit, Eugnostos the Blessed, and the Wisdom of Jesus Christ.

18. *El* means "god" in Hebrew. Compare the name Eleleth in other Sethian texts.

19. The names Yaldabaoth and Sakla are well known in other Sethian gnostic

texts; on Nebro, compare Nebruel in the Holy Book of the Great Invisible Spirit and Manichaean texts, as well as Nimrod in the Hebrew Bible (in the Greek of the Septuagint, Nebrod). The Gospel of Judas understands that the name Nebro/Nebrod/Nimrod means "rebel," and this may indicate an awareness of the possible meaning of the name in Hebrew.

20. Probably the signs of the zodiac.

21. Perhaps restore to read "who is the evil eye" or "who is the eye of fire."

22. Similar lists of angels are found in other Sethian texts. The correlation of Seth and Christ (here partially restored) is unusual in this context, and Harmathoth seems to be a composite name (Harmas + Athoth).

23. Or, "and the first ones are over chaos."

24. The following lines of translation are based on photographs of recovered fragments.

25. Perhaps restore to read "Israel" or "Istrael."

26. Restored.

27. The wandering stars are probably understood to be the five known planets (Mercury, Venus, Mars, Jupiter, and Saturn) plus the Moon.

28. The following lines of translation are based on photographs of recovered fragments.

29. The one who bears Jesus, here and below, is thought to be the fleshly, mortal body that supports the inner, spiritual person of Jesus for a period of time.

30. Perhaps restore to read "will all die," or the like.

31. As above, the man who bears Jesus is the mortal body that carries around the spiritual person of Jesus. According to Irenaeus of Lyon, the handing over of Jesus by Judas in the Gospel of Judas is a "mystery" through which things earthly and heavenly are thrown into dissolution. This description fits the text of the Gospel of Judas very well.

32. The song of Hannah, in 1 Samuel 2, employs very similar motifs (noted by Tage Petersen).

33. The following lines of translation are based on photographs of recovered fragments.

34. Jesus enters the light cloud, in what resembles a transfiguration or ascension account, and stars surround it, with the star of Judas in the lead.

35. The following lines of translation are based on photographs of recovered fragments.

36. Or, "they."

37. Here the meaning of Judas handing over Jesus to the authorities is

remarkably different from the accounts in the New Testament gospels. In the Gospel of Judas, when Judas hands Jesus over, the true, spiritual Jesus has already left, and as a result he will not die on the cross.

Chapter 4. The Secret Book of John

1. Coptic texts: Nag Hammadi Codex II,1: 1,1–32,10; III, 1: 1,1–40,11; IV,1: 1,1–49,28; Berlin Gnostic Codex 8502,2: 19,6–77,7. Citation: Irenaeus of Lyon, Against Heresies 1.29.1–4. The translation given here is based largely on the Coptic text of Nag Hammadi Codex II, which represents the longer version of the Secret Book of John.

2. Or, "a child" (Coptic *oualou,* in the shorter version in Berlin Gnostic Codex 8502; this must be restored in the Nag Hammadi Codex II version).

3. The father gazes into the water and falls in love with his own image in a manner that calls to mind Narcissus in Greek mythology (see Ovid, Metamorphoses 3.402–510). Through this love of the father for his own image, the father's thought (Coptic *ennoia,* from Greek) emanated, and the first thought or forethought (Coptic *pronoia,* from Greek) comes from the mind of the father: the divine mother, Barbelo. The father thus produces an entity independently, without the aid of a lover. Other gods who are credited with acts of independent procreation include the Greek god Zeus, who produces Athena, the daughter of Metis (wisdom or skill), from his head alongside the River (or Lake) Triton (see Hesiod, Theogony 886–900, 924–29), or the Egyptian god Atum, who mates with his hand and spits, that is, he produces the seed of life by means of masturbation.

4. Personified insight (*epinoia,* from Greek) plays a dominant role throughout the Secret Book of John. In Greek mythology the Titans Prometheos ("forethought") and Epimetheos ("afterthought," "insight") create human beings, though Epimetheos does his job imperfectly. Prometheos, who is linked to Athena, makes the humans stand upright, after the manner of the gods, and he takes fire from the gods and brings it down to earth. He thus functions as a savior of humans, but he is punished for his actions by being chained to a pillar in the mountains, where a bird of prey continually eats his liver. Eventually Herakles frees him. Much of this recalls aspects of the plot in the Secret Book of John, particularly the roles of forethought (*pronoia*), insight (*epinoia*), and the demiurge.

5. Sophia tries to imitate the original procreative act of the father. This account of Sophia bringing forth by herself seems to reflect ancient

gynecological theories about women's bodies and reproduction. In Greek mythology the goddess Hera also imitates Zeus and brings forth a child by herself. According to one version of the myth, the child is the monster Typhon (Homeric Hymn to Pythian Apollo 300–62). According to another, it is the lame deity Hephaistos, whom Hera evicts from Olympus and sends down to the world below (Hesiod, Theogony 924–29). Hephaistos, the artisan among the gods, is represented in Egypt by his counterpart Khnum, a ram-headed creator who molds creatures on a potter's wheel. In the Secret Book of John all the evils and misfortunes of this world derive from Sophia's blunder.

6. Or, "aborted fetus," as in Berlin Gnostic Codex 8502.

7. The scene recalls a noisy workshop in which a statue or a fetter is being forged.

8. The description of a human being and a shadow in a cave may well derive from the allegory of the cave in Plato's Republic, Book 7. The body as the prison or tomb of the soul is also a well-known Platonic and Orphic teaching.

9. The savior, here Jesus, is speaking.

10. Insight assumes the form of a tree, just as in Greek mythology Daphne changes into a laurel tree (see Ovid, Metamorphoses 1.452–562, and other gnostic texts, particularly On the Origin of the World). Like Daphne, insight is not to be apprehended, according to a later passage in the Secret Book of John.

11. The savior, here Jesus, is still speaking.

12. John is speaking.

13. The savior appears as a heavenly bird; the eagle is the bird of Zeus. Compare the Song of the Pearl, in which the royal letter flies as an eagle and becomes a voice of revelation.

14. Coptic *Eloim* and *Yawe,* two names of god in the Hebrew Bible. Elohim is a word that means "god" (literally "gods" since it is plural in form and ending), Yahweh is the name of god (based on the tetragrammaton, the ineffable four-letter name).

15. The water of forgetfulness recalls the water of the River Lethe in the Greek conception of the underworld. If a thirsty soul drinks of the water of this river, it forgets about its previous lives and thus may be reincarnated in another body.

16. The concluding hymn of the savior is found only in the longer version of the Secret Book of John. It reflects a hymn of *pronoia,* heavenly forethought, the divine mother, as savior. In the present Christianized version of the Secret Book of John the reader may understand the savior to be Jesus. In the hymn

the savior is described as coming down into the world in three descents, and a call to awaken to knowledge is addressed to a prototypical sleeper—that is, to any person who may be able to awaken to knowledge and salvation.

Chapter 5. On the Origin of the World

1. Coptic texts: Nag Hammadi Codex II,5: 97,24–127, 17; XIII,2: 50, 25–34 (fragment); British Library Oriental Manuscript 4926(1) (fragments). There is no title for the tractate in the manuscripts.
2. These opening lines are excerpted from the account of the creation of paradise in the text.
3. This being, the true human being, is Adam of light.
4. That is, Eve of Zoe.
5. The beast is the serpent in the story of Adam and Eve in paradise.
6. The song of Eve employs lines paralleled in the text Thunder.
7. This does not seem to follow what precedes it in the text.
8. Enlightened, exalted Eve escapes by changing into a tree, as in Greek mythology Daphne changes into a laurel tree (see Ovid, Metamorphoses 1.452–562, as well as the Secret Book of John).
9. The powers apparently ejaculate their semen into the mouth of earthly Eve.
10. The lesser day of rest is the Sabbath Day.
11. This seems to be a self-reference on the part of the author.
12. These lines are taken from the conclusion of the text.

Chapter 6. Thunder

1. Coptic text: Nag Hammadi Codex VI,2: 13,1–21,32.
2. Sophia.
3. Compare Eve, called Zoe, "life," in the Septuagint, the primal woman in the book of Genesis.

Chapter 7. The Gospel of Philip

1. Coptic text: Nag Hammadi Codex II,3: 51,29–86,19.
2. Or, "Sophia."
3. Partially restored.
4. Pleroma.

Chapter 8. The Gospel of Truth

1. Coptic text: Nag Hammadi Codex I,3: 16,31–43,24; XII,2: 57,1–60,30 (fragments).
2. Or, here and in the following lines, "the All," "the realm of all," that is, the universe derived from the divine.
3. Partially restored.
4. Or, perhaps, with Bentley Layton, "and surely then not because of the father" (continuing the negation from the previous clause).
5. Partially restored.
6. Partially restored.
7. Literally, "It."
8. Partially restored.
9. Or, "who is a mother to them" (Coptic *petoei ᵉmmeu neu*).

Chapter 9. The Secret Book of James

1. Coptic text: Nag Hammadi Codex I,2: 1,1–16,30.
2. The beginning of this paragraph incorporates minor restorations, and the entirety of this paragraph is difficult to translate. A significant distinction is made here between the spirit and the soul, as in Valentinian texts, and the right way to experience fullness—through spirit—is emphasized.
3. James.
4. Or, "rabbi" (Coptic *sah*).
5. The conclusion of the text describes the dispersal of the messengers (or apostles) to spread the message of Jesus throughout the world. James is based in Jerusalem, as the leader of the church there. The "loved ones who are to come" are future believers, like the very people reading the Secret Book of James. They are the children coming after James and Peter, and it is for their sakes that the revelation is given.

Chapter 10. The Round Dance of the Cross

1. Greek text: Acts of John 94–96.
2. The Round Dance of the Cross is said to have been taught by Jesus to his students just before his crucifixion.
3. Instructions for liturgical dance.

Chapter 11. The Book of Baruch

1. Greek text: Hippolytus of Rome, Refutation of All Heresies 5.24.1 and 37.1–3; 5.26.1–37 and 27.4.
2. Compare Herodotus, Histories 4.8–10. The ancient notion of a woman consisting of two parts, the virgin breasts above the waist and an animal temptation below, is contained in myths of the siren, a symbol of seduction and destruction in Homer's Odyssey.
3. *Edem* means "earth," and *Eden* means "paradise." Traditionally, *Eden* is said to be from the Hebrew *eden*, meaning "delight," or god's garden of delight. However, it is more probably related to a Sumerian word meaning "plain." The extant Greek text gives *edem*, as in the early Septuagint Greek translation.
4. Originally the Hebrew word for "gods," *Elohim* came to be normally translated "god" (singular) in Genesis 1:1, though elsewhere, as in the Psalms, it retains the plural notion of "gods."
5. Seven of the names of paternal angels are now lost.
6. This is Edem, Israel.
7. This is Elohim.

Chapter 12. The Song of the Pearl

1. Text: Acts of Thomas 108–13. The Song of the Pearl is preserved in a Greek version and a Syriac version. The translation here is based largely on the Greek version.
2. Not Babylon by the Euphrates but the Roman fortress city in present-day Old Cairo.
3. This understanding is based on the Greek version. In the Syriac version the letter, personified, simply speaks forth with its own voice.

Chapter 13. The Songs of Solomon

1. The Songs or Odes of Solomon are published in a Syriac version; several songs are also preserved in Coptic in the gnostic text Pistis Sophia.

Chapter 14. Poimandres

1. The text entitled Poimandres is Corpus Hermeticum I. The translation given here is from the Greek.
2. Logos.
3. Greek *pneuma,* "spirit" or "breath."
4. Greek *anthropos.*
5. That is, androgynous.
6. Or, "forethought" (Greek *pronoia*).

Chapter 15. The Ginza

1. The Ginza is preserved in texts written in Mandaic.

Chapter 16. Songs from the Mandaean Liturgy

1. These Songs from the Mandaean Liturgy are written in Mandaic.

Chapter 17. The Coptic Manichaean Songbook

1. Songs from the Manichaean Songbook are available in the Coptic edition of C. R. C. Allberry.
2. Stray beasts or dogs, a conjecture.
3. This song has many lacunae.

Chapter 18. The Great Song to Mani

1. The Great Song to Mani, a late piece of Manichaean poetry, was written in Turkish.
2. The cyclical process of metempsychosis, that is, the transmigration of the soul by way of rebirths and deaths, is called samsara. This transmigration extends from the lowest insect to the Brahma, the highest of the gods. The rank of one's new birth, after passing through a hell or a heaven, depends on one's karma in the previous life. In Sanskrit *samsara* means "the running around."

3. In Buddhism the five states of existence are those of gods, humans, hungry spirits (*pretas*), animals, and beings of hell.
4. This Buddhist "nirvana" is the Manichaean realm of light.
5. The Sumeru mountain is the central mountain of the universe in the Buddhist and Hindu cosmology.
6. The six organs of perception (*sadayatana*) in Buddhism are the five sense organs and *manas,* the mind.
7. The realm of light.
8. Probably Mani's Living Gospel.
9. The four Buddhas are probably Seth, Zoroaster, Buddha, and Jesus. "Four" is not in the original text.
10. The Buddhist Satan.
11. Mani's seven canonical books.

Chapter 19. The Mother of Books

1. The Mother of Books is available in a German translation published by Heinz Halm. The present English translation has been prepared from the German.
2. These and the following terms are the names of Arabic letters in the *Bismillah.*
3. The gnostic demiurge (for example, Yaldabaoth in the Secret Book of John) creates in a similar fashion in other texts.
4. Azazi'il's boastful statement recalls the arrogant claim of the demiurge in gnostic texts.
5. As the manifestation of the divine, Salman resembles Sophia, wisdom, or even the first human, in gnostic texts.
6. As noted before, he acts like the gnostic demiurge.
7. This claim may recall the Christian trinitarian confession.
8. These final passages describe how a person is liberated from the body and comes to wisdom, knowledge, and perfection.
9. Ten feast days to celebrate the martyrdom of Husayn.

Chapter 20. The Gospel of the Secret Supper

1. The Gospel of the Secret Supper is translated from the French edition of René Nelli.

2. In the Vienna version of the text a marginal note says that *ossop* is the same as the Valley of Josaphat, although the text reads "principle of fire."
3. That is, they were male and female.
4. The serpent's tail here suggests the penis.
5. The notion that Mary was inseminated through the ear is based on noncanonical apocrypha and is found in medieval painting. Here Jesus as an angel inseminates his mother the angel Mary with his sperm through her ear. This notion of purity is doubly reinforced, since Mary will not have been inseminated normally, and the child will issue from her pure ear rather than from her loins.

Chapter 21. A Nun's Sermon

1. A Nun's Sermon is translated from an anonymous poem in Provençal.

Epilogue

1. This is also the admonition inscribed on the temple of the Delphic Oracle, according to Plutarch.
2. Filoramo, *History of Gnosticism,* 145.
3. Rudolph, *Gnosis,* 275.
4. Second-century docetism (from Greek *dokein,* "to seem") affirmed Christ's divinity and scoffed at the idea that made Jesus both man and god.
5. The First Revelation of James, Codex V,3,15–20 (*Nag Hammadi Library,* 3d ed., p. 268).
6. The Second Discourse of Great Seth, Codex VII,2,56 (*Nag Hammadi Library,* 3d ed., p. 365).
7. The question of whether Jesus had two natures (human and divine) or one (divine) divided orthodox Christians and divergent sects for more than a thousand years. For example, in the sixth century the Byzantine emperor Justinian wavered, giving some leeway to the Monophysites, who taught that Jesus Christ was only divine. There were many sects who insisted on the docetic or monophysistic creed that Christ had only a divine nature, from the early Montanists, gnostics, and docetists to the tenth- and eleventh-century Bogomils in Constantinople and Bosnia, and their later Cathar adherents in northern Italy and southwestern France.

8. Grant, *Gnosticism and Early Christianity*, 19.

9. Ibid., 23.

10. Ibid., 26.

11. See Scholem for more on gnosticism as a self-centered religion in *Jewish Gnosticism*, 21ff.

12. Jonas, *Gnostic Religion*, 165–66.

13. Scholem, *Major Trends in Jewish Mysticism*, 14.

14. After distinguishing between spiritual leaps of the gnostic and others, we may note that these are descriptive, not evaluative, distinctions. The lives and poems of the sixteenth-century Spanish mystics Fray Luis de León and San Juan de la Cruz (Saint John of the Cross) have been and remain a lifelong summit.

15. In some main gnostic treatises Sophia, rather than the biblical god, creates the world and humans.

16. See Rudolph, *Gnosticism*, 25.

17. For a discussion of Hypatia see Mary R. Lefkowitz and Maureen Fant, *Women's Life in Greece and Rome*, 107–12.

18. In about 276 the Persian king Shapur I, at the behest of Zoroastrian clerics who felt threatened by the rise of Mani and the Manichaean gnostics, had Mani tried and executed. Yet some villages of Mandaeans survive even today in remote areas of Iran and Iraq.

19. Robinson, ed., *Nag Hammadi Library in English*.

20. Pagels, *Gnostic Gospels*, xx.

21. Robinson, ed., *Nag Hammadi Library in English*, 3.

22. Ibid., 4.

23. Ibid., 7.

24. Grant, *Gnosticism and Early Christianity*, 38.

25. "Confession of Baruch, once a Jew, then baptized and now returned to Judaism," translated by Nancy P. Stork of the English department at San Jose State University, found in the Jacques Fournier Register on the Jacques Fournier Home Page, http://www.sjsu,edu/depts/english/Fournier/Baruch.htm, pp. 1.10.

BIBLIOGRAPHY

Allberry, C. R. C. *A Manichaean Psalm-Book*. Stuttgart: W. Kohlhammer, 1938.

Arberry, A. J., ed. *The Koran Interpreted*. 2 vols. Spalding Library of Religion. London: Allen & Unwin, 1963.

Asin y Palacios, Michael. *Logia et agrapha Domini Jesu: Apud moslemicos scriptores, asceticos, praesertim, usitata, collegit, vertit, notis instruxit*. 2 vols. Turnhout, Belgium: Brepols, 1926–74.

Barnstone, Aliki, ed. *The Shambhala Anthology of Women's Spiritual Poetry*. Boston: Shambhala Publications, 2000.

————, and Willis Barnstone, eds. *A Book of Women Poets from Antiquity to Now*. New York: Schocken Books, 1980, 1992.

Barnstone, Willis. *The Other Bible*. San Francisco: Harper & Row, 1984.

————. *The Poetics of Translation: History, Theory, Practice*. New Haven, Conn.: Yale University Press, 1993.

————. *The Restored New Testament*. New York: Norton, 2009.

Barnstone, Willis, and Marvin Meyer, eds. *The Gnostic Bible*. 2d ed. Boston: Shambhala Publications, 2009.

————. *The Gnostic Bible: Book and Audio-CD Set*. Boston: Shambhala Publications, 2008.

Bauer, Walter. *Orthodoxy and Heresy in Earliest Christianity*. 2d ed. Philadelphia: Fortress Press, 1971.

BeDuhn, Jason. *The Manichaean Body: In Discipline and Ritual*. Baltimore: Johns Hopkins University Press, 2000.

Buckley, Jorunn Jacobsen. *The Mandaeans: Ancient Texts and Modern People*. Oxford, Eng.: Oxford University Press, 2002.

Culianu, Ioan Petru. "Gnosticism from the Middle Ages to the Present." In *The Encyclopedia of Religion*, edited by Mircea Eliade, 5.574–78. New York: Macmillan; London: Collier Macmillan, 1987.

_____. *The Tree of Gnosis: Gnostic Mythology from Early Christianity to Modern Nihilism.* Translated by H. S. Wiesner. San Francisco: HarperCollins, 1992.

De Boer, Esther A. *The Gospel of Mary: Beyond a Gnostic and a Biblical Mary Magdalene.* New York and London: Clark International, 2004.

Drower, Ethel S. *The Mandaeans of Iraq and Iran: Their Cults, Customs, Magic, Legends, and Folklore.* Oxford, Eng.: Clarendon Press, 1937.

Dunkerley, Roderic. *Beyond the Gospels.* Middlesex, Eng.: Penguin Books, 1957.

Festugière, A. J. *La Révélation d'Hermès Trismégiste.* 4 vols. Paris: Gabalda, 1949–54.

Filoramo, Giovanni. *A History of Gnosticism.* Oxford, Eng.: Blackwell, 1990.

Foerster, Werner, ed. *Gnosis: A Selection of Gnostic Texts.* Translated by R. McL. Wilson. 2 vols. Oxford, Eng.: Clarendon Press, 1974.

Grant, Robert M. *Gnosticism and Early Christianity.* 2d ed. New York: Columbia University Press, 1966.

H.D. *Trilogy.* Edited by Aliki Barnstone. New York: New Directions, 1998.

Haardt, Robert, ed. *Gnosis: Character and Testimony.* Leiden, Neth.: E. J. Brill, 1971.

Halm, Heinz. *Die islamische Gnosis: Die extreme Schia und die 'Alawiten.* Die Bibliothek des Morgenlandes. Zürich: Artemis, 1982.

Jeremias, Joachim. *Unknown Sayings of Jesus.* 2d ed. Translated by Reginald H. Fuller. London: S.P.C.K., 1964.

Jonas, Hans. *Gnosis und spätantiker Geist.* Part 1. 3d ed. FRLANT 51. Göttingen: Vandenhoeck & Ruprecht, 1964.

_____. *The Gnostic Religion: The Message of the Alien God and the Beginnings of Christianity.* 2d ed. Boston: Beacon Press, 1963.

Kasser, Rodolphe, Marvin Meyer, and Gregor Wurst, eds. *The Gospel of Judas.* 2d ed. Washington, D.C.: National Geographic Society, 2008.

Kasser, Rodolphe, Marvin Meyer, Gregor Wurst, and François Gaudard, eds. *The Gospel of Judas, Together with the Letter of Peter to Philip, James, and a Book of Allogenes, from Codex Tchacos: Critical Edition.* Washington, D.C.: National Geographic Society, 2007.

Khalidi, Tarif. *The Muslim Jesus: Sayings and Stories in Islamic Literature.* Cambridge, Mass.: Harvard University Press, 2001.

King, Karen L. "The Apocryphon of John: Part II of the Gospel of John?" Paper presented at the annual meeting of the Society of Biblical Literature, Denver, Colo., November 2001.

_____. *The Gospel of Mary of Magdala: Jesus and the First Woman Apostle.* Santa Rosa, Calif.: Polebridge Press, 2003.

_____. *What Is Gnosticism?* Cambridge, Mass.: Belknap Press/Harvard University Press, 2003.

Klimkeit, Hans-Joachim. *Gnosis on the Silk Road: Gnostic Texts from Central Asia.* San Francisco: HarperSanFrancisco, 1993.

Kloppenborg, John S. *Excavating Q: The History and Setting of the Sayings Gospel.* Minneapolis: Fortress Press, 2000.

Layton, Bentley. *The Gnostic Scriptures: A New Translation with Annotations and Introductions.* Garden City, N.Y.: Doubleday, 1987.

_____. "Prolegomena to the Study of Ancient Gnosticism." In *The Social World of the First Christians: Essays in Honor of Wayne A. Meeks,* edited by L. Michael White and O. Larry Yarbrough, 334–50. Minneapolis: Fortress, 1995.

Lidzbarski, Mark. *Ginza: Der Schatz oder das grosse Buch der Mandäer übersetzt und erklärt.* Göttingen, Ger.: Vandenhoeck & Ruprecht, 1925.

Lieu, S. N. C. *Manichaeism in the Later Roman Empire and Medieval China: A Historical Survey.* 2d ed. Tübingen: Mohr, 1992.

Lin Wu-shu. *Manichaeism and Its Spread to the East.* In Chinese; English review by P. Bryder in *Manichaean Studies Newsletter* 1 (1989): 15–19.

Mack, Burton L. *The Lost Gospel: The Book of Q and Christian Origins.* San Francisco: HarperSanFrancisco, 1993.

Mahé, Jean-Pierre, and Paul-Hubert Poirier, eds. *Écrits gnostiques.* Bibliothèque de la Pléiade. Paris: Gallimard, 2007.

Margoliouth, D. S. "Christ in Islam: Sayings Attributed to Christ by Mohammedan Writers." *The Expository Times* 5 (1893–94): 59, 107, 177–78, 503–504, 561.

Marjanen, Antti, ed. *Was There a Gnostic Religion?* Publications of the Finnish Exegetical Society 87. Helsinki: Finnish Exegetical Society; Göttingen: Vandenhoeck & Ruprecht, 2005.

Meyer, Marvin. "Did Jesus Drink from a Cup? The Equipment of Jesus and His Followers in Q and al-Ghazali." In *From Quest to Q: Festschrift James M. Robinson,* edited by Jon Ma. Asgeirsson, Kristin De Troyer, and Marvin W. Meyer, 143–56. Leuven, Belgium: Leuven University Press, 2000.

_____. *The Gnostic Discoveries: The Impact of the Nag Hammadi Library.* San Francisco: HarperSanFrancisco, 2005.

_____. *The Gospel of Thomas: The Hidden Sayings of Jesus.* San Francisco: HarperSanFrancisco, 1992.

_____. *Judas: The Definitive Collection of Gospels and Legends about the Infamous Apostle of Jesus.* San Francisco: HarperOne, 2007.

_____, ed. *The Nag Hammadi Scriptures: The International Edition.* San Francisco: HarperOne, 2007.

Mirecki, Paul A. "The Coptic Manichaean Synaxeis Codex: Descriptive Catalogue of Synaxeis Chapter Titles." In *Manichaean Studies: Proceedings of the First International Conference on Manichaeism*, edited by P. Bryder, 135–45. Lund Studies in African and Asian Religions 1. Lund, Sweden: Plus Ultra, 1988.

Nelli, René. *Écritures cathares; La Cène secrète; Le Livre des deux principes; Traité cathare; Le Rituel occitan; Le Rituel latin: Textes précathares et cathares présentés, traduits et commentés avec une introduction sur les origines et l'esprit du catharism.* New ed. Paris: Planète, 1968.

Nock, Arthur Darby, and A. J. Festugière, eds. *Corpus Hermeticum.* Paris: Sociéte d'édition "Les Belles lettres," 1945–54.

Pagels, Elaine H. *Beyond Belief: The Secret Gospel of Thomas.* New York: Random House, 2003.

_____. *The Gnostic Gospels.* New York: Random House, 1979.

Parrinder, Geoffrey. *Jesus in the Qur'an.* New York: Oxford University Press, 1965.

Patterson, Stephen J., James M. Robinson, and Hans-Gebhard Bethge. *The Fifth Gospel: The Gospel of Thomas Comes of Age.* Harrisburg, Pa.: Trinity Press International, 1998.

Pearson, Birger A. *Ancient Gnosticism: Traditions and Literature.* Minneapolis: Fortress Press, 2007.

_____. *Gnosticism and Christianity in Roman and Coptic Egypt.* Studies in Antiquity and Christianity. New York and London: Clark International, 2004.

Robinson, James M., ed. *The Nag Hammadi Library in English.* 3d ed. San Francisco: HarperSanFrancisco, 1988.

Robinson, James M., Paul Hoffman, and John S. Kloppenborg, eds. *The Critical Edition of Q: Synopsis Including the Gospels of Matthew and Luke, Mark, and Thomas with English, German, and French Translations of Q and Thomas.* Leuven, Belgium: Peeters, 2000.

Robinson, James M., and Helmut Koester. *Trajectories through Early Christianity.* Philadelphia: Fortress Press, 1971.

Robson, James. *Christ in Islam.* The Wisdom of the East. London: Murray, 1929.

Ropes, James Hardy. "Agrapha." In *A Dictionary of the Bible*, edited by James Hastings, ex. vol., 343–52. New York: Scribner's; Edinburgh: T. & T. Clark, 1904.

Rudolph, Kurt. *Gnosis: The Nature and History of Gnosticism.* Translated by R. McL. Wilson. San Francisco: Harper Collins, 1983.

_____. *Die Mandäer. Vol. 1. Prolegomena: Das Mandäerproblem. Vol. 2. Der Kult.* Göttingen: Vandenhoeck & Ruprecht, 1960–61.

Schenke, Hans-Martin, Hans-Gebhard Bethge, and Ursula Ulrike Kaiser, eds. *Nag Hammadi Deutsch.* 2 vols. Die Griechischen Christlichen Schriftsteller der ersten Jahrhunderte, Neue Folge, 8, 12. Berlin and New York: Walter de Gruyter, 2001, 2003.

Schneemelcher, Wilhelm, ed. *New Testament Apocrypha.* English translation edited by R. McL. Wilson. 2 vols. Cambridge: James Clarke; Louisville, Ky.: Westminster/John Knox, 1991–92.

Scholem, Gershom. *Jewish Gnosticism, Merkabah Mysticism, and Talmudic Tradition.* New York: Jewish Theological Seminary of America, 1960.

Scholer, David M. *Nag Hammadi Bibliography, 1948–1969.* Nag Hammadi Studies 1. Leiden, Neth.: E. J. Brill, 1971.

_____. *Nag Hammadi Bibliography, 1970–1994.* Nag Hammadi Studies 32. Leiden, Neth.: E. J. Brill, 1997.

Schweitzer, Albert. *The Quest of the Historical Jesus: A Critical Study of Its Progress from Reimarus to Wrede.* Translated by W. Montgomery. New York: Macmillan, 1968.

Segal, Alan F. *Two Powers in Heaven: Early Rabbinic Reports about Christianity and Gnosticism.* Studies in Judaism and Late Antiquity 25. Leiden, Neth.: E. J. Brill, 1977.

Turner, John D. *Sethian Gnosticism and the Platonic Tradition.* Bibliothèque de Nag Hammadi, Section "Études" 6. Sainte-Foy, Québec: Presses de l'Université Laval; Louvain, Belgium: Peeters, 2001.

Williams, Michael A. *Rethinking "Gnosticism": An Argument for Dismantling a Dubious Category.* Princeton: Princeton University Press, 1996.